Structuralism:

Theory and Practice

Jean Duffy

Lecturer in French,
University of Sheffield

UNIVERSITY of GLASGOW FRENCH AND GERMAN PUBLICATIONS 1992

University of Glasgow French and German Publications

Series Editors: Mark G. Ward (German)
                   Geoff Woollen (French)

Consultant Editors : Colin Smethurst
                     Kenneth Varty

Modern Languages Building, University of Glasgow,
Glasgow G12 8QL, Scotland.

First published 1992.

Printed by Castle Cary Press, Somerset BA7 7AN.

ISBN   0 85261 319 9

Contents

Preface

In the course of the last two or three decades, numerous general guides
to structuralism have been written and there has been a steady growth in
the body of critical works applying the theory to individual texts.
Notwithstanding these contributions, the teaching of structuralism to
undergraduate students has remained a problem, not least because of the
dearth of publications that offer an introduction to the theory together
with practical exercises which could be carried out in class. In recent
years, a number of theoretical and practical textbooks have been
produced for teachers and students of English literature. Teachers and
students of French, however, have had to make do with rather more
piecemeal material, usually lectures accompanied by extensive handouts
and bibliographies which are both expensive and time-consuming to
produce. The aim of this introduction is to eliminate at least some of the
problems that will be encountered by those who wish to offer a course
on structuralism.

Inevitably, I have had to be extremely selective both in the choice of
theoretical models discussed and the textual examples chosen. The
criteria of selection have been intelligibility and familiarity. The
theoretical discussion is based on those models which I have found to be
most accessible to the undergraduate, while my examples and exercises
have been chosen from texts which the student is likely to encounter in
the course of an undergraduate degree programme.

Inevitably, too, it has not been possible to pursue some of the more
far-reaching or radical implications of certain concepts and models.
Thus the contribution of Barthes's reading of *S/Z* to deconstructive
debate and post-structuralist redefinitions of intertextuality has not been
discussed. More advanced students should, obviously, be encouraged to
address the more sophisticated issues raised by the models.

The guide may obviously be used in a number of ways, but it is
hoped that, with the current emphasis on student-centred learning, it
could, at least in part, supplant hand-out-dominated lectures and
encourage seminar debate. Ideally, the theoretical material would be
studied by the student in his or her own time, the exercises then
constituting the basis of class discussion, seminar papers and submitted
essays.

I should like to thank Roger Hawkins, who first drew my attention to
the usefulness of linguistics-based concepts in the analysis and
interpretation of Apollinaire's poem *Le Voyageur*, Éditions Gallimard,
for permission to reproduce it, and Geoff Woollen—*toi, l'Auvergnat*.

Jean Duffy   Sheffield, November 1991

Chapter One

Saussure

'It is Saussure who stands behind the claim, which many people would today espouse, that to study man is essentially to study the various systems by which he and his cultures organize and give meaning to the world.'[1] So concludes Jonathan Culler's excellent introduction to the theory and intellectual legacy of Ferdinand de Saussure, the father of modern linguistics and the forerunner of modern literary theory. Few of the many books on critical approaches or literary theory published in the last two decades omit reference to Saussure, the Swiss linguistician and thinker, whose theories on language underpin modern semiology.

> The importance of Saussure lies not simply in his contribution to linguistics *per se,* but in the fact that he made what might otherwise have seemed a recondite and specialised discipline a major intellectual presence and model for other disciplines of the 'human sciences'.[2]

In particular, semiologists are indebted to Saussure for the key distinctions between signifier and signified, between *langue* and *parole,* and between paradigm and syntagm which inform structuralist analyses of literature and other phenomena.

For Saussure, one of the fundamental weaknesses of earlier linguistic studies was their omission to define precisely the nature of language. Nineteenth-century analysis 'ne s'est jamais préoccupée de dégager la nature de son objet d'étude. Or, sans cette opération élémentaire, une science est incapable de se faire une méthode.'[3] Saussure's answer to this problem of definition was that language is a system of signs. Language distinguishes itself from expressive natural noise by its conventionality, by its capacity to communicate ideas, and by its social and interpersonal dimension:

> [La langue] est à la fois un produit social de la faculté du langage et un ensemble de conventions nécessaires, adoptées par le corps social pour permettre l'exercice de cette faculté chez les individus. (p. 25).

Saussure's analysis of the nature of the linguistic sign led him to an equally challenging conclusion, which undermined all conceptions of language as a nomenclature or inventory of linguistic units. The linguistic sign, he argued, unites not a thing and a name but a concept and a sound-image. The sign is composed of two elements—the signifier

---

[1] Jonathan Culler, *Saussure* (Glasgow: Fontana/Collins, 1976), p. 117.

[2] Culler, *op. cit.,* p. 53.

[3] *Cours de linguistique générale* (Paris: Payot, 1968), p. 16.

and the signified—and the relationship between the two is arbitrary, conventional, and unmotivated. The signifier is the vocal or graphological form which signifies, while the signified is the concept signified. The relationship between the signifier (*signifiant*) and the signified (*signifié*) is unmotivated in that '[le signifiant est] arbitraire par rapport au signifié, avec lequel il n'a aucune attache naturelle dans la réalité' (p. 101). Thus there is no inherent reason why the item of furniture which we call *table* is not called *chair* and vice versa. Onomatopoeic words are the exceptions which by their paucity prove the rule. Furthermore, as Saussure points out, the 'natural' link between signifier and signified in onomatopoeic words becomes increasingly tenuous as they are subjected to the phonetic and morphological changes affecting other words.

If, as Saussure argues, the relationship between signifier and signified is arbitrary, how then do we communicate, how is meaning produced? We are able to communicate, he argues, because language is an interpersonal, social system of relations and differences. Meaning is a product of phonic, graphological and conceptual differences among the components of the linguistic system. Thus in speech, phonic difference enables us to distinguish a given word from all the others in the system:

> Puisqu'il n'y a point d'image vocale qui réponde plus qu'une autre à ce qu'elle est chargée de dire, il est évident, même *a priori*, que jamais un fragment de langue ne pourra être fondée, en dernière analyse, sur autre chose que sur sa non-coïncidence avec le reste. *Artitraire et différentiel* sont deux qualités corrélatives. (p. 163)

Similarly, in writing it is difference which carries signification: 'les valeurs de l'écriture n'agissent que par leur opposition réciproque au sein d'un système défini, composé d'un nombre déterminé de lettres' (p. 165). Thus on a very simple level, it can be argued that the meanings of the following words are derived to a large extent from minimal vocal and graphological differences:

bat	bat	bad
cat	bet	bag
fat	bit	ban
pat	but	bar
hat		bat

On a conceptual level, the 'contenu [d'un mot] n'est vraiment déterminé que par le concours de ce qui existe en dehors de lui' (p. 160). Saussure explains his reasoning by a comparison with currency. The value of a coin is determined by two factors: firstly, by the fact that it can be exchanged for a fixed quantity of something dissimilar (e.g. bread, meat, etc.); secondly, by the fact that it can be compared with another unit in the same system (e.g. a fifty-pence coin compared with a pound) or with units of a different system (e.g. a U.S. dollar, a French franc, etc.). Hence his conclusion that values are always made up:

> 1° par une chose *dissemblable* susceptible d'être *échangée* contre celle dont la valeur est à déterminer;
> 2° par des choses *similaires* qu'on peut *comparer* avec celle dont la valeur est en cause (p. 159).

To illustrate his argument, Saussure points to the way in which near synonyms limit each other's value reciprocally: 'des synonymes comme *redouter, craindre, avoir peur* n'ont de valeur propre que par leur opposition; si *redouter* n'existait pas, tout son contenu irait à ses concurrents' (p. 160). Similarly, the conceptual value of the word 'aimer' is determined and limited by its differential and associative relationships with 'affectionner', 'chérir', 'adorer' and 'idolâtrer'. The absence of a straight exchange value between the words of one language and another further illustrates and corroborates his argument. Individual languages divide up the conceptual plane in different ways. Thus English learners can be frustrated to find that the French word 'louer' means both 'to let' and 'to rent', while the verb 'to know' is translated by the French 'connaître' or 'savoir' in different contexts (Saussure, p. 161; Culler, p. 21)..

So far our discussion of language and meaning has been limited to the analysis of the individual linguistic unit and its differential relationships with the other units in the system. Communication, however, is not simply based on the exchange of individual linguistic units, but involves the selection and combination of numerous units into sequences of varying length. This brings us to Saussure's distinction between *langue* and *parole*, between the 'somme d'empreintes déposées dans chaque cerveau' (p. 38) and the instances of linguistic execution. *Langue* is the body of forms from which the individual selects in producing a particular instance of *parole*. In distinguishing between *langue* and *parole*, Saussure is distinguishing between, on the one hand, the social and essential and, on the other, 'les manifestations [...] individuelles et momentanées' (*ibid.*). Every time the individual speaker formulates a phrase, a sentence, a paragraph or a text, he is involved in a double process: the selection of units from among all the possible units in the system, and their combination in a linear chain. The relationships among the units in individual instances of *parole* are designated

'syntagmatic' by Saussure. The term 'syntagmatic' relates to the
sequential and combinatory relationships of discourse. The relationships
among the units of the langue from which a selection is made are
designated 'associative' (by Saussure) or 'paradigmatic' (by later
linguists and semiologists). Within the *langue* any word will be 'comme
le centre d'une constellation, le point où convergent d'autres termes
coordonnés, dont la somme est indéfinie' (p. 174). Each word in the
langue will have a multitude of phonic, morphological, and conceptual
relationships with other words. By contrast, the word used in an
instance of *parole* will be defined by its relationships with what precedes
and follows it in the discursive chain. Thus on the paradigmatic axis, the
word 'cat' is phonically related to 'car', 'cab', 'bat' etc. and conceptually
to 'moggy', 'mouser', 'pussy', 'lion', etc. In the syntagm 'She fed the cat
regularly', the word 'cat' contributes to the production of meaning by
virtue of its differential relationships with other units in the sequence (a
noun rather than a verb or an adverb; the object rather than the subject)
and its capacity to be combined with these other units in a conceptually
coherent sequence (contrast, for example, 'She fed the mat regularly').

Now while any *parole* that is primarily concerned with economy and
clarity of communication will, if it is successful, result in syntagmatic
combinations which are both syntactically and conceptually coherent,
the same cannot always be said of the poetic or literary text. Indeed,
much twentieth-century analysis of the literary is founded on the
premise that literary language deviates from or indeed violates linguistic
norms and promotes rereading as opposed to consumption. This
premise, arguable and contentious though it is, will inform the rest of
this chapter, which will focus more closely on the usefulness of the
distinction between syntagmatic and paradigmatic relations in the
analysis of the literary text.

Literary deviance can clearly take many different forms and can
vary enormously in degree. Part of the critic's job is therefore to
determine the nature and the intensity of the deviance. A first reading of
a poem or piece of literary prose will usually act as a rough guide to the
intelligibility of the piece. However, if the reader or critic wishes to go
beyond this impressionistic level, an analysis of the text (i.e. an instance
of *parole*) which scrutinizes paradigmatic selection and syntagmatic
combination will not only give a more accurate measure of literary
deviance, but may offer crucial indicators of theme and subject matter.
The steps which one may take in the analysis of a piece of literature will
vary in number and order, according to the complexity and length of
the passage or text. The following model analysis of Guillaume
Apollinaire's poem *Le Voyageur* [4] is offered as an example of one
possible interpretive route and the sort of questions which one might
fruitfully ask oneself when attempting to elucidate it.

[4] *Alcools* (1913). © Éditions GALLIMARD, reproduced by kind permission.

Le Voyageur

A Fernand Fleuret

OUVREZ-MOI cette porte où je frappe en pleurant

La vie est variable aussi bien que l'Euripe

Tu regardais un banc de nuages descendre
Avec le paquebot orphelin vers les fièvres futures
5   Et de tous ces regrets de tous ces repentirs
    Te souviens-tu

Vagues poissons arqués fleurs surmarines
Une nuit c'était la mer
Et les fleuves s'y répandaient

10   Je m'en souviens je m'en souviens encore

Un soir je descendis dans une auberge triste
Auprès de Luxembourg
Dans le fond de la salle il s'envolait un Christ
Quelqu'un avait un furet
15   Un autre un hérisson
L'on jouait aux cartes
Et toi tu m'avais oublié

Te souviens-tu du long orphelinat des gares
Nous traversâmes des villes qui tout le jour tournaient
20   Et vomissaient la nuit le soleil des journées
O matelots ô femmes sombres et vous mes compagnons
    Souvenez-vous-en

Deux matelots qui ne s'étaient jamais quittés
Deux matelots qui ne s'étaient jamais parlé
25   Le plus jeune en mourant tomba sur le côté

    O vous chers compagnons
Sonneries électriques des gares chant des moissonneuses
Traîneau d'un boucher régiment des rues sans nombre
Cavalerie des ponts nuits livides de l'alcool
30   Les villes que j'ai vues vivaient comme des folles

Te souviens-tu des banlieues et du troupeau plaintif des paysages

Les cyprès projetaient sous la lune leurs ombres
J'écoutais cette nuit au déclin de l'été
Un oiseau langoureux et toujours irrité
35   Et le bruit éternel d'un fleuve large et sombre

Mais tandis que mourants roulaient vers l'estuaire
Tous les regards tous les regards de tous les yeux
Les bords étaient déserts herbus silencieux
Et la montagne à l'autre rive était très claire

40
Alors sans bruit sans qu'on pût voir rien de vivant
Contre le mont passèrent des ombres vivaces
De profil ou soudain tournant leurs vagues faces
Et tenant l'ombre de leurs lances en avant

45
Les ombres contre le mont perpendiculaire
Grandissaient ou parfois s'abaissaient brusquement
Et ces ombres barbues pleuraient humainement
En glissant pas à pas sur la montagne claire

50
Qui donc reconnais-tu sur ces vieilles photographies
Te souviens-tu du jour où une abeille tomba dans le feu
C'était tu t'en souviens à la fin de l'été
Deux matelots qui ne s'étaient jamais quittés
L'aîné portait au cou une chaîne de fer
Le plus jeune mettait ses cheveux blonds en tresse

Ouvrez-moi cette porte où je frappe en pleurant

55
La vie est variable aussi bien que l'Euripe

Stage one: the 'impressionistic' reading

On a first reading, it may be useful to try to relate the text to the following scales:

1. Literal Intelligibility:

/	/	/	/	/
Easy	Difficult in places	Fairly difficult	Difficult	Incomprehensible

2. Anticipated number of readings necessary to understand, identify the subject:

/	/	/	/
One	Two	Several	Many

3. Extent of deviation from everyday, functional usage:

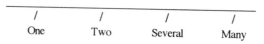

/	/	/
Low	Moderate	High

Le Voyageur: This is clearly a poem which resists interpretation even after several readings, and which would seem to deviate markedly from everyday linguistic usage.

Stage Two:

Looking at the poem as an instance of *parole,* identify the features which disrupt the syntagmatic sequence and the linear production and reception of meaning, for example: syntactical complexities; uncertainties; aberrations; mistakes; logical problems; absence or misuse of coordinating and subordinating conjunctions; non-standard punctuation; apparent redundancies such as repetition, parallelism etc; allusions which need to be investigated, etc.

Le Voyageur: A fairly early reading of the poem will reveal not only a change in verse pattern and rhythm between lines 32 and 47, but also a greater coherence in the syntax. If we relate this formal element to the content of the poem, lines 32-47 clearly offer a fairly sustained evocation of a single image, which contrasts with the many disruptions of syntax and the fragmentation of the first 31 lines. This change is clearly significant, though difficult to interpret fully at this stage.

A more detailed analysis of the language of the first 31 lines shows various types of syntagmatic disruption. The syntax seems frequently to break down: words are often simply listed; grammatical status of words is not always clear. There are numerous logical and chronological problems: words, phrases, entire lines seem to be juxtaposed without explanation, coordination or subordination. There is a lack of subordinating conjunctions which might clarify the relationships between elements or help us to establish a hierarchy among elements. There is no punctuation or clear demarcation of the beginning and end of sense units. There are a number of apparent redundancies: the opening lines are repeated at the end of the poem; certain phrases are repeated in the body of the poem. The allusions to 'L'Euripe' and to Christ require elucidation.

Stage Three:

As the reader tries to interpret texts presenting such a high degree of difficulty, a close examination of individual units may provide a point of entry into the logically impenetrable. The establishment of lexical sets or groups of associated words can help identify key concepts.

Le Voyageur: The word 'voyageur' is related, on the paradigmatic axis
of language to words such as 'voyage', 'mouvement', 'variété',
'changement', 'temps'. A quick scan of the lexical sets of the poem will
confirm the relevance of these associations:

Movement:	descendre (3), paquebot (4), s'envolait (13), gares (18), traversâmes (19), tournaient (19) tomba (25), roulaient (36), passèrent (41), tournant (42), s'abaissaient (45), tomba (49).
Variety:	variable (repeated at beginning and end of poem, therefore important).
Change:	'tu regardais un banc de nuages descendre' (3) 'en mourant tomba sur le côté' (25).
Time:	futures (4), regrets (5), souviens (*passim*) nuit (8), soir (11), tout le jour (19), nuits (29), cette nuit (33), jour (49), été (33), été (50).

A tentative interpretation of the broad lines of the poem can be made
at this stage by correlating the connotations of recurrent words and
concepts. A first working hypothesis might read: the poem is 'about' the
journey of life. The multiple, disjointed images which characterise the
first half of the poem are the varied experiences and memories of the
speaker. This hypothesis is strengthened by the repetition of the word
'souvenir'. The multiple graphic images are fragments of the past. This
very broad, universalising interpretation is further supported by the
occurrence of words from other lexical sets:

> the four elements: air (nuages), water (mer, fleuve),
>   fire (feu), earth (montagne, mont).

> references to the sun and the moon.

> references to day and night.
> references to the city and the countryside.

> references to various types of animal, fish, insect, bird and
>   plant life.

Notwithstanding the support given to the thesis that the poem is 'about'
life and its variety, numerous interpretive problems remain. This
hypothesis does not account, for example, for the occurrence of words

relating to sickness ('fièvres' 'vomissaient'), emotional or psychological distress ('pleurant', 'regrets', 'repentirs', 'folles', 'plaintif', 'irrite', 'pleuraient', 'triste') and the references to death or dying.

The recurrence of such words and in particular of words relating to death forces a revision of our initial hypothesis that this is a poem about life. Conceptually, of course, the word 'life' defines itself differentially or negatively in relation to the word 'death'. Life implies its opposite. Once again, confirmation that death is a feature of the poem is to be found elsewhere:

in the associations of the words 'orphelin' (4), 'orphelinat' (18), 'tomba' (25),'boucher' (28), 'livides' (29), 'déclin' (33),'sombre' (35), 'fin' (50).

in the recurrence of words taken from military vocabulary: 'régiment' (28), 'cavalerie' (29), 'lances' (43). While the word 'matelot' conjures up a life of adventure and variety, military vocabulary has much closer associations with death.

in the reference to cypress trees. It was a custom among the ancients to plant cypress trees round their graves. The cypress was also one of the trees which, reputedly, formed the wood of the Cross.

in the allusion to Euripos. The Euripos is a 'narrow strait in the Aegean Sea, between the Greek island of Euboea (Evoia) and the mainland of Central Greece...It has strong tidal currents... which reverse seven or more times a day. According to popular tradition, the philosopher Aristotle, in despair at his inability to solve the problem of their cause, drowned here.'[5]

in the reference to Christ who died and rose again and who continues to do so in representation after representation, as in this 'auberge triste'.

Stage Four:

At this point, we can perhaps return to an earlier problem: that of the discrepancy between the fragmentation and disrupted syntax of the first 31 lines and the much greater coherence of lines 32-47. Here it could be argued that lines 1-31 offer concrete examples of the 'variable', while lines 32-47 develop in a much more sustained manner the concept of the 'living dead'. The relative coherence/incoherence of

---

[5] *Encyclopaedia Britannica*, entry on 'Euripus'.

the syntagmatic chain reflects the function of the images in the thematic development. Lines 32-47 constitute a much more homogeneous and coherent sequence, and could be seen almost as a poem within a poem, which sheds new light on the fragments of memory which precede and follow. This sequence slows down the erratic pace of the first 31 lines and inhibits progression in the 'narrative' of the journey through life. However, within the sequence, relationships of chronology, coordination, subordination and conjunction are more clearly marked ('et', 'mais', 'tandis que', 'et', 'alors', 'sans que', 'où', 'et', 'et', 'en'). The greater clarity of the syntax, the more homogeneous nature of the visual image and the extension of the image over twelve lines signal the sequence as the thematic centre of the poem. This is, for the speaker, literally the most 'haunting' image.

Stage Five:

The recognition of the association between life and death and the development of the concept of 'living death' in lines 32-47 make us reassess the speaker's situation and look not only at his past but also his present. We are led to posit new hypotheses. Perhaps the traveller has come to the end of his journey, reached what he hopes will be his final destination. Perhaps his repeated apostrophe is a plea to be released from the living death of memory. Perhaps, like the bee which, doomed to die at the end of the summer, goes forward to meet death in the fire, he wishes to forestall death.

Stage Six:

One final substantial disjunction remains to be interpreted: the oscillation between 'tu' and 'vous' forms in the various apostrophes which punctuate the poem and which interrupt the syntagmatic progression. The identity of the 'vous' is fairly easy to establish; its meaning is limited by the reference to the speaker's 'chers compagnons': fellow-travellers, those encountered on his journey and now behind the door of death. The meaning of the 'tu' is less clearly established by context. Lines 23-25 suggests one possibility: the 'tu' refers to a particularly close companion who died young. Alternatively, perhaps the addressee is a younger self with whom the addresser is trying to communicate. Lines 51-53 leave both possibilities open, but establish a physical difference between the two 'matelots'. Here, we must ask ourselves whether these lines are purely descriptive or whether the selection and differentiation of physical features are significant. Difference, of course, in Saussurian terms is the key to the production of meaning. The associations of the phrases 'chaîne de fer' (imprisonment, slavery) and 'cheveux blonds en tresse' (youth, beauty) can be related to some of the hypotheses already made. The speaker (the older of the two 'matelots', the older self) is imprisoned in a life full of sombre memories; the addressee (the younger 'matelot', the younger self) has in death retained his beauty and youth.

Exercises

1. (a)   Identify in *Le Voyageur* examples of the following features and comment on the ways in which they disrupt syntagmatic progression and promote paradigmatic association: parallelism, puns, synonyms/near-synonyms, antithesis, incongruity, ellipsis, parataxis, accumulation, inversion, metaphor, simile.

   (b)   Comment on the role of phonic difference and association in *Le Voyageur*.

2.   Comment on the relationship between syntagm and paradigm in the following passage from Claude Simon's *La Route des Flandres* (Éditions de Minuit, pp. 22-3):

> Et de nouveau il me semblait voir cela: se détachant sur le vert inimitable des opulents marronniers, presque noir, les jockeys passant dans le tintement de la cloche pour se rendre au départ, haut perchés, simiesques, sur les bêtes graciles et élégantes, leurs casaques multicolores se suivant dans les pastilles de soleil, comme ceci: Jaune, bretelles et toque bleues — le fond vert noir des marronniers — Noire, croix de Saint-André bleue et toque blanche — le mur vert noir des marronniers — Damier bleu et rose toque bleue — le mur vert noir des marronniers — Rayée cerise et bleue, toque bleu ciel — le mur vert noir des marronniers — Jaune, manches cerclées jaune et rouge, toque rouge — le mur vert noir des marronniers — Rouge, coutures grises, toque rouge — le mur vert noir des marronniers — Bleu clair, manches noires, brassard et toque rouges — le mur vert noir des marronniers — Grenat, toque grenat — le mur vert noir des marronniers — Jaune, cercle et brassards verts, toque rouge — le mur vert noir des marronniers — Bleue, manches rouges, brassard et toque verts — le mur vert noir des marronniers — Violette, croix de Lorraine cerise, toque violette — le mur vert noir des marronniers — Rouge, pois bleus, manches et toque rouges — le mur vert noir des marronniers — Marron cerclé bleu ciel, toque noire... les casaques étincelantes glissant, le mur vert sombre des feuilles, les casaques étincelantes, les pastilles de soleil dansant, les chevaux aux noms dansants — Carpasta, Milady, Zeida, Naharo, Romance, Primarosa, Riskoli, Carpaccio, Wild-Risk, Samarkand, Chichibu — les

jeunes pouliches posant l'un après l'autre leurs sabots délicats et les retirant, comme si elles se brûlaient, dansant, semblant se tenir, suspendues et dansantes, au-dessus du sol, sans toucher terre, la cloche, le bronze tintant, n'en finissant plus de tinter, tandis que l'une après l'autre les chatoyantes casaques glissaient silencieusement dans l'élégant après-midi.

3.   To what extent do the concepts of syntagm and paradigm facilitate the analysis of the following?

Baudelaire's *Correspondances*.
Mallarmé's *Brise marine*.
Rimbaud's *Après le déluge*.
Michaux's *The Thin Man*.
Prévert's *Câble confidentiel*.

The first four of these poems can be found in C.A. Hackett (ed.), *Anthology of Modern French Poetry* (Oxford: Blackwell, 1964), pp. 2, 22, 57, 163. The Prévert poem is published in C. Mortelier (ed.), *Anthologie Prévert* (London: Methuen, 1981), pp. 109-110.

Chapter Two

Structuralism

The history of the development of structuralist theory has been written many times over the last two decades. Its debt to Formalism, the way it has been superseded by deconstruction, and its many internal arguments and inconsistencies have been analysed in detail by numerous commentators. The history of structuralism, its effects upon a wide range of disciplines and the nuances of its internal debates lie outside the scope of the present study. Our purpose in this chapter is to isolate certain key concepts constituting the common foundations for many quite different structuralist approaches which have survived the process of diversification and transformation that has taken place within structuralism since the nineteen-sixties.

The Code

As we saw in the first chapter, the concept of language as a system of signs has profound implications for the study of meaning-production. Saussure himself saw linguistics as part of a much greater science of semiology, but he accords language a privileged position because:

> rien n'est plus propre que la langue à faire comprendre la nature du problème sémiologique.[1]

The early structuralist theorists responded to Saussure's invitation with ingenuity and enthusiasm. The anthropologist Claude Lévi-Strauss took the lead. In *Anthropologie structurale,* he asked a fundamental question:

> Nous sommes conduits, en effet, à nous demander si les divers aspects de la vie sociale (y compris l'art et la religion)—dont nous savons déjà que l'étude peut s'aider de méthodes et de notions empruntées à la linguistique—ne consistent pas en phénomènes dont la nature rejoint celle même du langage.[2]

The linguistic model seemed to offer a model for the analysis of culture in general. Lévi-Strauss's investigation of the sophisticated codes which operate within apparently primitive cultures revealed the extent to

---

[1] *Cours de linguistique générale,* p. 34.

[2] *Anthropologie structurale* (Paris: Plon, 1958), p. 71.

which all societies construct their reality, in particular through the media of myth and art:

> For the student of literature, the implications of Lévi-Strauss's sort of 'structural' anthropology and the structural linguistics from which it derives, must be considerable.[...] This view enables us to see 'civilized' works of art as, in great measure, linked with 'primitive' mythology in their concern to reinforce and uphold the same process: the *construction* of the world they appear only to describe. [...] It thus strengthens the notion that art acts as a *mediating*, moulding force in society rather than as an agency which merely reflects or records.[3]

Following Lévi-Strauss's initiative, literary critics began to look beyond the surface randomness and diversity of art in search of generalised structures and patterns. Critics like Roland Barthes, Gérard Genette and Philippe Hamon began to look at the ways in which man encodes reality through literature.

However, literature is not just the product of other codes; it is itself a signifying system which structures, patterns and encodes the larger linguistic system upon which it depends. Literature is seen to function, not as an innocent reflector of the world but as an elaborate system of codes:

> The codes act as agencies—whether we are conscious of them or not—which *modify, determine* and most importantly, *generate* meaning—in a manner far from innocent, far from untrammelled, and very much closer to the complicated ways in which language itself imposes its own mediating, shaping pattern on what we think of as an objective world 'out there'.[4]

Literature, like language, is seen to stand in a problematical relationship with reality. Both literature (the corpus of texts) and the literary work are systems with their own codes and structures, their own procedures of differentiation and association, in short, their own means of meaning-production.

Reality, realism and convention

One of the central notions which has survived the fragmented and diverse evolution of structuralist theory is the premise—based initially on anthropological analysis—that 'nature' and 'reality' are in fact cultural constructs:

---

[3] Terence Hawkes, *Structuralism and Semiotics* (London: Methuen, 1977), pp. 55-6.

[4] *Ibid.*, p. 110.

> 'Reality' [...] needs to be understood not as an absolute and immutable
> given but as a production within which representation will depend on (and
> dialectically contribute to) what the French Marxist theoretician Louis
> Althusser has described as 'practical ideology', a complex formation of
> montages of notions, representations, images and modes of actions,
> gestures, attitudes, the whole ensemble functioning as practical norms
> which govern the concrete stance of men in relation to the objects and
> problems of their social and individual existence; in short, the lived
> relationship of men to their world. In this sense, the 'realistic' is not
> substantial but formal (a process of significant 'fictions'), and, in
> connection with the novel, it may be described in the notion of the
> *vraisemblable* of a particular society, the generally received picture of what
> may be regarded as 'realistic'; such a *vraisemblable* being founded in our
> own culture by, amongst other things, the novel itself.[5]

Clearly, such an argument has profound consequences for the way in
which the structuralist critic approaches art and literature. The equation
of reality with human construct and realism with convention strikes at
the heart of the mimetic assumptions underlying most traditional forms
of criticism. The view that literature and art represent or reflect the
social, natural or psychological world is undermined, and critical labels
such as 'realistic' or 'realism' immediately become problematical. The
so-called 'realistic' work can be said simply to be corroborating or
complying with a contemporary and relative definition of reality. Thus
the omniscient narrator of nineteenth-century realist fiction can be seen
as the product of a positivist optimism which believed in man's ability to
know, understand, and control his world. By contrast the development
of multiple narrative perspectives and fragmented narrative forms can
be seen as a symptom of twentieth-century neurosis, uncertainty, and
relativism.

In their early polemical attempts to undermine mimetic assumptions,
structuralist theorists and critics showed little mercy towards the classics
of the nineteenth century and, piece by piece, set about dislodging the
corner-stones of realism. In his essay 'Vraisemblance et motivation',[6]
Gérard Genette demonstrates the way in which Balzac disguises the
improbabilities of his fictional world by a barrage of heavy-handed
narrative devices. Repeatedly the exceptional or specific is explained by
reference to some 'general rule' coined, of course, by Balzac. The often
profound cracks in his *Weltanschauung* are papered over by personal
theories which support his own plots:

> Balzac, on le sait, a 'des théories sur tout', mais ces théories ne sont pas là
> pour le seul plaisir de théoriser, elles sont d'abord au service du récit: elles
> lui servent à chaque instant de caution, de justification, de *captatio
> benevolentiae,* elles bouchent toutes ses fissures, elles balisent tous ses
> carrefours. (p. 81)

---

[5] Stephen Heath, *The 'Nouveau Roman'* (London: Elek, 1972), p. 20.

[6] *Figures II* (Paris: Seuil, 1969), pp. 71-99.

The privileged psychological insight into character which the
Balzacian narrator offers the reader is a means of rendering credible
the 'invraisemblable' of his world view:

> Moins évidentes mais plus nombreuses et au fond plus importantes, les
> interventions qui portent sur la détermination des conduites, individuelles et
> collectives, et qui montrent la volonté de l'auteur de conduire l'action, coûte
> que coûte, dans telle direction et non dans telle autre. [...] On voit que 'la
> lumière psychologique' a bien pour fonction [...] de conjurer
> l'invraisemblable en révélant—ou en supposant—les *liens*, les *nœuds*, les
> *attaches* qui assurent tant bien que mal la cohérence de ce que Balzac nomme
> l'ordre moral. (pp. 81-2)

It is the Flaubertian description which comes under close scrutiny in
Barthes's essay 'L'Effet du réel'. The descriptive set-piece of the
nineteenth-century novel, by its isolation and staticism within the mobile
temporal structure of the text, begs a crucial question:

> Tout, dans le récit, est-il signifiant, et sinon, s'il subsiste dans le syntagme
> narratif quelques pages insignifiantes, quelle est en definitive, si l'on peut
> dire, la signification de cette insignifiance?[7]

Barthes shows that the realist novel is peppered with apparently
insignificant details and redundancies, which resist thematic
interpretation and whose function is to bolster the referential illusion
and to equate sign with referent:

> If the basic convention governing the novel is the expectation that readers
> will, through their contact with the text, be able to recognize a world which
> it produces or to which it refers, it ought to be possible to identify at least
> some elements of the text whose function it is to confirm this expectation
> and to assert the representational or mimetic orientation of fiction. At the
> most elementary level this function is fulfilled by what one might call a
> descriptive residue: items whose only apparent role in the text is that of
> denoting a concrete reality (trivial gestures, insignificant objects,
> superfluous dialogue). [...] The pure representation of reality thus becomes,
> as Barthes, says, a resistance to meaning, an instance of the 'referential
> illusion', according to which the meaning of a sign is nothing other than its
> referent.[8]

In 'Un discours contraint',[9] Philippe Hamon carries out one of the
fullest inventories of the conventions and devices employed in
nineteenth-century fiction to make the reader believe that it is copying
reality. Among these Hamon cites the explanatory flash-back, the
incorporation of visual supports (e.g. family trees, illustrations), the
elaboration of 'typical', recognizable scenes which establish a character

---

[7] *Littérature et réalité*, ed. G.Genette and T. Todorov (Paris: Seuil, 1982), pp. 81-90 (p. 83).

[8] J. Culler, *Structuralist Poetics* [*SP*] (London: Routledge and Kegan Paul, 1975), pp. 192-3.

[9] *Poétique*, 16 (1973), 411-54; reprinted. in *Littérature et réalité*, pp. 119-81.

within a specific socio-professional sphere, the inclusion of character-specialists who by implication demonstrate the technical knowledge of the author and the delegation of narration to a character-witness.

Naturalisation

Literary language, according to structuralists, is distinguished from communicative language by a number of features—by its deferral of meaning, its formal organisation, its apparent autonomy and its permanence. Barthes argues in *Le Degré zéro de l'écriture* that writing has an intimidating monumentality which is denied the spoken language. The primary function of literary writing is not to inform, explain or give direct access to an imaginary world; rather 'elle manifeste une essence et menace d'un secret, elle est une contre-communication, elle intimide'.[10] Writing is distinguished from communicative language by the fact that it always seems to be 'symbolique, introversée, tournée ostensiblement du côté d'un versant secret du langage' (p. 18). When we open a literary text, we confront an intimidating body of writing which demands interpretation rather than consumption or passive acceptance.

The impulse to interpret and to reduce the intimidation of the text is strong. As Jonathan Culler points out 'the urge to assimilate that power and permanence or to let that formal organization work upon us requires us to make literature into a communication, to reduce its strangeness, and to draw upon supplementary conventions which enable it, as we say, to speak to us' (*SP*, p. 134). Naturalisation or recuperation is the process by which we make sense of the words on the paper, make them correspond to something with which we are familiar, in particular to cultural and literary models which we know. Naturalisation is a complex process which operates at a number of levels as we try to assimilate the text and render it intelligible. As readers, we are constantly drawing upon a wide range of sense-giving sources—our own experience, a repertoire of cultural norms, technical knowledge, conventions relating to genre, symbolic archetypes and myths, etc. As we draw on these multiple areas of competence, we try to detect significant, intellectually coherent patterns among the apparently disparate and discrete elements of the text.

Every culture has, for example, its own body of accepted knowledge about human behaviour, natural phenomena, destiny, life in general. This knowledge manifests itself in a multitude of ways: proverbs, maxims, myths, superstitions, clichés, stereotypes and so on. While we may be very sceptical about this workaday 'knowledge', it remains an important element of our cultural baggage which the writer can exploit

[10] *Le Degré zéro de l'écriture* (Paris: Seuil, 1972 [1953]), p. 18.

in laying the foundations of his fictional world.

The conventions of genre perform an important function in the naturalisation of a text. Our willingness to suspend disbelief varies considerably according to the type of text which we are reading; for example, our tolerance and credulity when we read science fiction or a tale of the supernatural are clearly much greater than when we read a social realist or psychological novel. It is clear from these variations that genre acts as a delimiting framework within which the process of naturalisation takes place.

> The function of genre conventions is essentially to establish a contract between writer and reader so as to make certain relevant expectations operative and thus to permit both compliance with and deviation from accepted modes of intelligibility. (*SP*, p. 147)

Thus, the conventions of the picaresque novel and our consequent expectations of it tolerate the most unlikely coincidences, narrow escapes and concentrated sequences of events, while the behavioural novel eliminates explicit narratorial commentary in favour of the telling and significant moment. The classic detective novel is established upon the premise that 'the truth will out':

> The detective story is a particularly good example of the force of genre conventions: the assumption that characters are psychologically intelligible, that the crime has a solution which will eventually be revealed, that the relevant evidence will be given but that the solution will be of some complexity, are all essential to the enjoyment of such books. (*SP*, p. 148)

Symbolic naturalisation comes into play when other more obvious—logical, causal, deterministic—explanations are absent or inadequate. Once again, the reader's competence and cultural baggage are crucial. The writer may be relying upon time-honoured symbolic associations which identify certain colours, objects or creatures with quite specific abstract meanings. Thus, typical signifiers of purity would be the colour white or the lily, while the colour red or an exotic blossom might signify sensuality.

In early structuralist criticism, naturalisation received a rather bad press, largely as Culler points out, because of 'a desire to avoid premature foreclosure, to allow the text to differentiate itself from ordinary language, to grant maximum scope to the play of formal features and of semantic uncertainties' (*SP*, p. 160) Fiction which resisted naturalisation, such as the *nouveau roman*, was revered, partly no doubt because it showed the same clinical and critical understanding of the conventions of nineteenth-century fiction as structuralism. In contrast, nineteenth-century fiction was seen to be mechanistic and rather easily dismantled. Thus, in 'Un discours contraint', Philippe Hamon demonstrates the impatience of the realist text. Hamon argues that the narrative can be schematised into 'une dialectique de classes logiques complémentaires' (*Littérature et réalité*, p. 160) which regulates the production of meaning. In the production of meaning the writer plays upon these dialectic relationships, varying the distance between the two poles according to whether he wishes to accelerate naturalisation or to defer meaning. Such relationships relate to the posing of questions and the supply of answers, statements of appearance and revelation of reality, statements relating to the virtual and the actualisation of the virtual, the establishment of plans of action and their realisation, the naming of a character and his or her description, and so on. The writer who wishes to impede recuperation, delay revelation, and maintain suspense will maximise the textual distance between the complementary elements of the text. It is Hamon's contention that the realist novel rejects such procedures in favour of a 'sémantisation accélérée' (*ibid.*), i.e. an immediate investment of intelligible meaning in the elements of the narrative. Thus, the naming of a character in Balzac will usually be followed by a body of information including biographical, physical and psychological data, examples of characteristic behaviour and a plan. Plans tend to be put into action quickly; references to virtual behaviour are confirmed by actual behaviour; causes have immediate effects.

Hamon's thesis is undoubtedly verifiable on many occasions in nineteenth-century fiction. However, the mechanistic approach to realist and naturalist fiction and to 'mimetic' fiction in general has, in more recent years been challenged by a number of critical studies which have looked beyond the more obvious and laborious nineteenth-century conventions and found often surprising points of resistance and problems of interpretation. Thus, Christopher Prendergast can write of *Le Pere Goriot:*

> The 'truth' of the novel is consciously, even aggressively, posited as a challenge to the *doxa*, as functioning outside, in opposition to the established conventions of the *vraisemblable*. [...] The novel cannot be painlessly absorbed (digested) into the corpus of pre-existing, ready-made significations.[11]

The Author and the Reader

The rejection by post-Saussurian linguisticians of a one-to-one, referential relationship between word and meaning has far-reaching implications, not least of which is the challenge it makes to traditional assumptions about the relationship between the author and the work. If the writer is working within a system in which meaning is produced

---

[11] *Balzac: Fiction and Melodrama* (London: Edward Arnold, 1978), p. 186.

through differentiation and association, then his control over the meanings produced in the combination of linguistic units is seriously undermined. Hence Barthes's polemical paradox that 'c'est le langage qui parle, ce n'est pas l'auteur'.[12] Hence too the rejection by structuralists of the author-centred approach whereby the reader or critic seeks to explain the text by reference to the author's biography, by the correlation of evidence on his opinions, interests or psyche, and by speculation about his intention(s). In his controversial essay 'La Mort de l'auteur', Barthes perfunctorily dismisses such approaches:

> L'image de la littérature que l'on peut trouver dans la culture courante [...] est tyranniquement centrée sur l'auteur, sa personne, son histoire, ses goûts, ses passions. (p. 62)

With structuralism, the author loses his authority, is displaced from his dominant position in criticism and becomes himself 'a creature of paper' or an 'effect of language'. Once the text enters the public domain, the author's control over it ceases, and the job of meaning-production passes to the reader.

> Once a text is in circulation the umbilical cord, so to speak, between author and text is cut and the text leads an independent existence.[...] The 'multiplicity' of meanings which make up a text is focused not on the author, but on the reader.[13]

The activity of reading as Barthes outlines it in the early pages of *S/Z* is a demanding one and makes no concession to consumerism or dogmatism. Interpretation is neither a question of receiving pre-existing meaning or of conferring a single, definitive meaning upon the text. Reading is a painstaking graduated process of finding and reviewing meaning. Finding meanings is to name them, to articulate what the work is about, but as the reader progresses through the text, these names will give way to other names. In short, reading is a tireless process of approximation and revision in which the reader neither consumes nor imposes meaning but participates in its production through an appreciation of the text's plurality of meanings:

> Interpréter un texte, ce n'est pas lui donner un sens (plus ou moins fondé, plus ou moins libre); c'est au contraire apprécier de quel pluriel il est fait.[14]

This appreciation of multivalence, according to Barthes, explains the activity of rereading. In rereading, the reader's prime concern is not the establishment of the 'vrai' text or some definitive truth, but rather the encounter with 'le texte pluriel, même et nouveau' (p. 23).

---

[12] 'La Mort de l'auteur', in *Le Bruissement de la langue* (Paris: Seuil, 1984), pp. 61-9.

[13] R. Webster, *Studying Literary Theory: An Introduction* (London: E. Arnold, 1990), p. 19.

[14] *S/Z* (Paris: Seuil, 1970), p. 11.

Given the foregoing premises, it is not surprising that structuralism offered the reader a new status with regard to the text. With structuralism, the reader assumes a central role hitherto denied him, and the reading process, its assumptions, strategies and creative potential are examined and categorised. Barthes's *S/Z* can be seen as a meticulous, sustained account of the reading process rather than a piece of criticism on a Balzacian short story.

The idea that reading is a parasitic complement to the creative activity, or that it performs a purely reactive function in relation to a given text, is rejected outright. On the contrary, the reader plays a crucial, active role in the production of meaning; indeed it is the reader who becomes:

> l'espace même ou s'inscrivent, sans qu'aucune ne se perde, toutes les citations dont est faite une écriture; l'unité d'un texte n'est pas dans son origine, mais dans sa destination, mais cette destination ne peut plus être personnelle: le lecteur est un homme sans histoire, sans biographie, sans psychologie; il est seulement ce *quelqu'un* qui tient rassemblées dans un même champ toutes les traces dont est constitué l'écrit.[15]

In the opening pages of *S/Z*, Barthes draws a distinction between what he calls the *lisible* and the *scriptible* (usually translated as 'readerly' and 'writerly'). In using these terms one must exercise great care. Culler rightly points out that they are not taxonomical, i.e. classificatory, labels which one can simply attach to a particular text; rather they are the poles of a theoretical model relating to degrees of intelligibility. The text which is predominantly *lisible* is a variation on a well-established pattern, corresponds to and satisfies the expectations which the reader has derived from his familiarity with the 'classics' of previous ages. The role of the reader here is more or less restricted to that of passive consumption; he reacts by accepting or rejecting the text, but he does not participate in the production of meaning. The term *scriptible* refers to an ideal text which would indefinitely resist interpretive reduction and closure. The reader's role here would approximate to that of the writer; he would be in a position to 'jouer lui-même, [...] d'accéder pleinement à l'enchantement du signifiant, à la volupté de l'écriture' (*S/Z*, p. 10). The *scriptible* is the positive co-ordinate in Barthes's model precisely because it acknowledges the role of the reader in the 'game' of meaning-production:

> Pourquoi le scriptible est-il notre valeur? Parce que l'enjeu du travail littéraire (de la littérature comme travail), c'est d'en faire du lecteur, non plus un consommateur, mais un producteur du texte. Notre littérature est marquée par le divorce impitoyable que l'institution littéraire maintient entre le fabricant et l'usager du texte, son propriétaire et son client, son auteur et son lecteur. Ce lecteur est alors plongé dans une sorte d'oisiveté,

---

[15] 'La Mort de l'auteur', pp. 66-7.

d'intransitivité, et, pour tout dire, de *sérieux:* au lieu de jouer lui-même d'accéder pleinement à l'enchantement du signifiant, à la volupte de l'écriture, il ne lui reste plus en partage que la pauvre liberté de recevoir ou de rejeter le texte: la lecture n'est plus qu'un *referendum.* En face du texte scriptible s'établit donc sa contre-valeur, sa valeur négative, réactive: ce qui peut être lu, mais non écrit: le *lisible.* (*ibid.*)

In practical terms, Barthes's model explores the distinction between, on the one hand, popular fiction and texts which have become 'classics', and on the other, texts which run counter to literary expectations and which resist interpretation in terms of established critical practices and criteria. Thus, despite the obvious parallels between Balzac's *Eugénie Grandet* and Nathalie Sarraute's *Portrait d'un inconnu* (1956), the former tends towards the *lisible* while the latter tends towards the *scriptible.* Though Barthes clearly promotes the *scriptible* as a critical criterion, he acknowledges that any text, if it is to engage the reader, must be neither totally *lisible* nor totally *scriptible.* Even the most avant-garde, disruptive text must take account of the reader's tolerance, requires some mimetic dimension. Thus, in the work of writers such as Claude Simon or Robbe-Grillet, the play of meaning upon meaning takes place within a broadly intelligible framework; even the *nouveau roman* has a 'subject', the 'aventure de l'écriture'. By the same token, the text which is more or less *lisible* is not simply a predictable reworking of an established novelistic formula. If it is to continue to engage readers its meaning should not be obvious, predictable and fixed. Its survival depends on a certain degree of plurality. It should, therefore, come as no surprise that, as Jonathan Culler points out, 'when structuralists write about classical texts they end up by discovering gaps, uncertainties, instances of subversion and other features which it is rather too easy to consider as specifically modern' (*SP*, p. 191). Given this coexistence within the literary text of the *lisible* and the *scriptible,* it becomes clear that Barthes's model relates less to evolution and the 'classicisation' of the previously innovatory than to a dynamic tension—which is essential to literature—between elements which are readily understood and naturalised and those which resist understanding and naturalisation.

Intertextuality

The question of intertextuality is a complex and vexed one. Defined broadly, intertextuality refers to the concept whereby literature is itself seen as a signifying system, within which the individual text functions as an instance of *parole* defining itself in relation to all the other texts or instances of *parole.* The concept of intertextuality clearly has its origins in a number of other structuralist assumptions. If one accepts that language is a system into which we are all born, the elements of which we select, combine and recombine in speech and writing, then notions such as creativity, inventiveness and originality become relative terms which must be understood within the context of the inevitably derivative nature of all instances of *parole*. Secondly, intertextuality also relates to the view that all perception and all conceptions of 'reality' are channelled through a variety of cultural codes. This is a view shared by structuralist critics and by the writers of the *nouveau roman*. Both groups argue that one of the most important cultural codes—partly because, being written down, it survives in a way that the spoken word does not—is literature. Every writer and reader is to some extent seeing the world through the literature of previous generations and the activities of writing and reading take place within the context of literary tradition. Thus the written word carries the imprint of previous usage and the meanings are produced and interpreted in relation to an infinite body of previous productions and interpretations. Thirdly, the promotion of the text as system invalidates the author-centred approach and invites a relational conception of the work, one that demands the recognition of meaningful links with other texts and maximises the number of potential interpretations.

Of the many theoretical works which have tackled this difficult issue, Laurent Jenny's article 'La Stratégie de la forme' is one of the most accessible. In it, Jenny argues that intertextuality is related to but not reducible to such familiar critical practices as source-research and the study of influences. Intertextuality is at once more wide and more precise in its definition. Viewed as a general literary phenomenon, intertextuality is all-encompassing in that every literary work is seen to have an incalculable number of intertextual relationships with the incalculable and ever-increasing number of texts which make up the literary system. Viewed as a mechanism of literary production, intertextuality is seen to be more precise than concepts such as 'influence'. As Jenny points out, 'l'intertextualité désigne non pas une addition confuse et mystérieuse d'influences, mais le travail de transformation et d'assimilation de plusieurs textes opéré par un texte centreur qui garde le *leadership* du sens'.[16]

Literary production becomes then, to use Roger Webster's phrase 'a kind of discursive recycling' (*op. cit.*, p. 97). The text rewrites other texts, combines elements from other texts into new patterns. Intertextuality may be formal or thematic and it serves a variety of functions within the system of the individual text. On the thematic level it could be argued that literature deals over and over again with the same set of themes (love, hatred, sex, war, time, space, family, etc.). Clearly such an argument is rather banal and much too general to be

---

[16] 'La Stratégie de la forme', *Poétique*, 27 (1976), 257-81 (p. 262).

useful. However, in many cases it is fairly easy to identify conscious
thematic relationships between a work and quite specific works within
the intertextual system. Thus, Claude Simon's novel *Le Vent* (1957) is a
reworking of Dostoievski's novel *The Idiot*. Moreover, in its
exploration of the ways in which representation invests meaning in and
imposes pattern on the apparently random and discrete, *Le Vent* also
draws upon a wide range of Biblical allusion. The epigraph is another
commonly found example of intertextuality. In *Le Vent*, the epigraph
provides a point of access to the central themes of the novel and warns
the reader of the danger, not only of disorders but also of order. The
alert reader will recognise the distortions produced by the narrator's
attempts to render intelligible and coherent his amorphous data.

The functions of intertextual play are many and varied. Explicit or
recognizable references to analogous situations in other texts may serve
to corroborate the 'reality effect' through parallelism and
generalisation. They may also seek to strengthen the author-reader
contract by establishing the common cultural ground between them.
Intertextuality has also frequently been put to polemical use. Parody and
satire are notable examples of what Jenny calls 'le détournement
culturel'. Intertextuality becomes a means of challenging the canon, of
undermining the instituted:

> Son rôle c'est de re-énoncer de façon décisive des discours dont le poids est
> devenu tyrannique. Discours clinquants, discours fossiles...Redire pour
> cerner, clore dans un autre discours, plus puissant donc. Parler pour
> oblitérer. Ou bien patiemment, dénier pour dépasser. (p. 279)

More interestingly, perhaps, intertextual play can also serve to
reactivate the 'original' text and to enrich and multiply the meanings of
the new text. Intertextuality works against stagnation, because the
removal of a passage from its original context and its transposition
creates around it a network of new, unforeseen connotations. The
function of intertextuality in such cases is to 'mettre en lumière les
syntagmes figées (les "mythologies') ankylosés dans les phrases, se
distancier par rapport à leur banalité en les outrant et enfin dégager le
signifiant de sa gangue pour le relancer dans un nouveau procès de
signification. [...] La relance de la signification intervient en même
temps que toute nouvelle mise en contexte' (p. 279). Commenting on
Michel Butor's reworking of Chateaubriand in *6,810,000 litres d'eau
par seconde* (1965), Jenny proposes a dizzying perspective on the logical
implications of such intertextual play:

> On peut ainsi explorer la charge sémantique virtuelle d'un texte, mettre à la
> fois l'accent sur les points clés de sa structuration et sur le caractère ouvert
> de cette structure, sur son infinité potentielle [...] qui est aussi celle de
> l'infinité des contextes possibles. (p. 280)

Moreover, as layer upon layer of intertextual reference is superimposed one upon the other, the text becomes the point of encounter of historically distant but mutually enriching *paroles:*

> Quels que soient les textes assimilés, le statut du discours intertextuel est ainsi comparable à celui d'une super-parole en ceci que les constituants de ce discours ne sont plus des mots, mais du déjà parlé, du déjà organisé, des fragments textuels. L'intertextualité parle une langue dont le vocabulaire est la somme des textes existants. (p. 266)

Formal intertextuality is seen when a work takes up and re-uses a device or structure which is a recognisable feature of another work, or of a particular type of literature or genre. Thus, in *Aucassin et Nicolette,* the long description recounting Aucassin's preparation for battle and the donning of his armour parodies similar standard accounts in the *chanson de geste*. Nor is formal intertextuality restricted to isolated devices. The entire fabric of a work may be underpinned by an archetypal structure belonging to another genre. Thus, the *nouveau roman* adopts, only to subvert, the investigatory structure of the detective novel. The ingenuous reader falls into trap after trap, assembles and correlates unreliable clues and evidence, only to find that no solution or 'truth' is forthcoming.

Intertextuality makes of the text a multi-dimensional space, in which linear progression is dislocated, naturalisation inhibited and interpretive closure prevented in favour of semantic play. Intertextual play is the 'rejet définitif du point final qui pourrait clore le sens et figer la forme' (p. 280). Illusionism and the mimetic conception of literature are undermined, since the text is seen to refer not to reality, but to past representations, to the previously written. The search for the source or original stimulus for a text is seen to lie not in the author's life or psyche but in other texts. Hence the importance of generative intertextuality in the *nouveau roman*. In the generation of new texts, Claude Simon draws on an immense range of other works on which he effects a variety of subversive, transformative and creative activities. Simon's work also exemplifies what Jean Ricardou calls 'intertextualité restreinte', that is, intertextual play within the corpus of texts written by a particular writer. Many passages of Simon's works have their source in passages of his earlier works. Ricardou's concept of restricted intertextuality can be seen as a way of retaining the notion of the specificity of the literary *œuvre,* though he insists that this approach should not be viewed as a return to the author-centred approach. In Ricardou's scheme of things the author is reduced to a signature which is the mark of the 'ensemble particulier' of the *œuvre:*

Se satisfaire de la seule intertextualité générale serait commettre une erreur: l'effacement d'un ensemble particulier, celui des textes portant la même signature. Or, c'est aussi par rapport aux textes marqués du même nom, *et cela de façon spécifique,* que les textes s'écrivent. Claude Simon ne sera donc pas considéré comme un auteur, mais comme un écrivain produisant des textes par rapport aux textes qu'il a signés, c'est-à-dire comme un scripteur pris dans des problèmes *d'intertextualité restreinte.*[17]

Ricardou's rider to the more ambitious discussion of intertextuality offers a less intimidating and perhaps more realistic point of entry to the analysis of the play among texts, and allays the misgivings of readers and critics who have profound reservations about biographical approaches, but who are reluctant to see the demise of the *œuvre.*

Exercises

1. Explain the way in which the letter which opens *L'Immoraliste* facilitates naturalisation of the tale which follows.

2. Find examples from nineteenth-century fiction to illustrate the various items in Hamon's inventory of devices used to corroborate the illusionism or reality effect of the novel.

3. There are many passages in *Illusions perdues* in which Balzac flaunts his 'technical knowledge'. Can you identify them and their function in the text?

4. To what extent do conventions of genre facilitate naturalisation in the following:

  (a) *La Chanson de Roland.*

  (b) *Phèdre.*

  (c) *Candide.*

  (d) *Le Grand Meaulnes.*

5. To what extent does Robbe-Grillet's novel *Dans le labyrinthe* flout conventions of genre and resist recuperation?

---

[17] '"Claude Simon" textuellement', *Colloque de Cérisy: Claude Simon,* ed. J. Ricardou (Paris: U.G.E., 1975), 7-19 (p. 11).

6.   'Dans le programme réaliste, le monde est descriptible, accessible
     à la dénomination. Par là, il s'oppose au monde du discours
     fantastique (l'innommable, l'indescriptible, le monstre...); ce
     programme se caractérise aussi par la volonté d'exhaustivité (le
     discours fantastique est souvent, lui, partiel et parcimonieux), et
     le réel est alors envisagé comme un champ complexe et
     foisonnant, discontinu, 'riche' et nombrable, dénommable, dont il
     s'agit de faire l'inventaire' (Hamon, 'Un discours contraint').
     Discuss the validity of this statement, illustrating it with examples
     from realist and fantasy fiction.

7.   Comment on the intertextual relationship between Camus's *Le
     Malentendu* and the following passage from *L'Étranger* (II. ii,
     Folio ed., pp. 124-5), paying due attention to the ways in which
     the 'original' text has been transformed, and to the semantic play
     between the two texts.

> Entre ma paillasse et la planche du lit, j'avais trouvé, en effet, un vieux
> morceau de journal presque collé à l'étoffe, jauni et transparent. Il
> relatait un fait divers dont le début manquait, mais qui avait dû se passer
> en Tchécoslovaquie. Un homme était parti d'un village tchèque pour
> faire fortune. Au bout de vingt-cinq ans, riche, il était revenu avec une
> femme et un enfant. Sa mère tenait un hôtel avec sa sœur dans son
> village natal. Pour les surprendre, il avait laissé sa femme et son enfant
> dans un autre établissement, était allé chez sa mère qui ne l'avait pas
> reconnu quand il était entré. Par plaisanterie, il avait eu l'idée de prendre
> une chambre. Il avait montré son argent. Dans la nuit, sa mère et sa
> sœur l'avaient assassiné à coups de marteau pour le voler et avaient jeté
> son corps dans la rivière. Le matin, la femme était venue, avait révélé
> sans le savoir l'identité du voyageur. La mère s'était pendue. La sœur
> s'était jetée dans un puits. J'ai dû lire cette histoire des milliers de fois.
> D'un côté, elle était invraisemblable. D'un autre, elle était naturelle. De
> toute façon, je trouvais que le voyageur l'avait un peu mérité et qu'il ne
> faut jamais jouer.

Chapter Three

Semiology and Characterisation

Characterisation has come under particularly close scrutiny in the work of Philippe Hamon, whose seminal theoretical essay 'Pour un statut sémiologique du personnage'[1] has been followed by a meticulous structuralist analysis of characterisation in Zola.[2] Hamon's conception of characterisation is both very ambitious and limited. Drawing upon the work of Claude Bremond and A. J. Greimas,[3] Hamon produces a multifacetted model which acknowledges the semiological status of the character and which demands an analysis of the entire system of characterisation within a given novel or series of novels. For all its sophistication, the heavy dependence of Hamon's model on taxonomical classification makes it unsurprising that the assumed norm underlying many of his arguments is realist and naturalist characterisation. The insights which Hamon offers into nineteenth-century fiction are well founded; the assumptions upon which his model rests inevitably restrict the viability of its application to modernist and post-modernist texts, though it remains highly useful in measuring deviation in modern texts that parody or subvert realist or naturalist technique.

In his introductory remarks to 'Pour un statut sémiologique du personnage', Hamon argues that, despite the ostensible prominence given by critics to the characters of fiction, characterisation remains a poorly-understood dimension of literature. While acknowledging that the concept of 'character' cannot be totally divorced from a more general conception of the person, he also points out, with considerable justification, that the results of much psychologically based analysis are vague and high speculative. Hamon seeks not to replace more traditional approaches; but rather to impose on them a greater rigour by making them follow, and therefore depend on, a semiological analysis. The character should be seen not as a *donnée,* but as a sign functioning within a textual system. Hamon goes on to remind us that the character is a unit within a 'textual grammar', that the function of character can be assumed by inanimate phenomena and that the character is as much a reconstruction produced by the reader as a construction of the text.

---

[1] *Littérature*, 6 (1972), 86-110, reprinted in *Poétique du récit*, ed. G. Genette and T. Todorov (Paris: Seuil, 1977), pp. 115-80.

[2] *Le Personnel du roman: le système des personnages dans les 'Rougon-Macquart' d'Émile Zola* (Geneva: Droz, 1983).

[3] For further discussion of Bremond and Greimas, see Culler, *Structuralist Poetics*, respectively pp. 208-11; 75-95.

Having in a sense suspended humanist preconceptions about the character, Hamon establishes the linguistic foundations of his own model. The latter has its origins in the semiological division of signs into three basic categories:

1. *Referential* signs, that is, signs which relate to external reality (table, giraffe, Picasso, river, etc.) or to a concept (structure, apocalypse, freedom), and which have stable dictionary definitions.

2. *Deictic* signs, that is, signs which refer to and signal a particular instance of enunciation. First and second person pronouns, demonstratives and certain spatial and temporal adverbs—e.g. here, now, tomorrow—fall into this category. The meaning of these signs is not stable, but derived from their use in a specific instance of discourse.

3. *Anaphoric* signs, that is, signs which refer back or forward to other signs used in the same speech act. Third person pronouns and substitutional verbs such as 'faire' and 'do' belong to this category. The meaning of signs is variable within the text and their function is cohesive and economical in that they decrease the cost of the message.

Likewise, characters can be divided into three basic categories, though, as Hamon points out, the one character may fall into different categories at different points in the narrative:

1. *Personnages-référentiels.* This category encompasses historical figures, mythological characters, allegorical embodiments, and social types. These characters all have an instituted meaning within a culture and their interpretation depends upon the reader's participation in and understanding of that culture. They function as referential anchors, consolidating the 'reality effect' and verisimilitude of the work, and refer to the 'grand Texte de l'idéologie, des clichés, ou de la culture' ('Pour un statut', p. 122) In certain genres—e.g. the medieval romance—the identification of the social type automatically permits the identification of the hero.

2. *Personnages-embrayeurs.* These characters serve to signal the presence of the author, the reader or their delegates within the text, and include spokesmen, choruses, interlocutors, and artistic characters. Thus the narrator of Gide's *L'Immoraliste* who has listened to Michel's tale is at one and the same time an author figure, in that he has recorded Michel's oral account, and a reader, in that as a listener, he, like us, has been presented with an unresolved dilemma of interpretation. The concluding sections of Constant's *Adolphe,* in which two opposing moral evaluations of the foregoing tale are expounded, stand as potential

readings and challenge the reader to attempt to select between them or to find a means of reconciling them.

3. *Personnages-anaphores*. These characters weave a network of internal allusions across the text, establish connections among separate sections and narrative series. They serve to organise and unify, and include characters who predict, recall, confess or confide, and who make plans. Thus in the concluding chapter of *Candide*, the old woman poses an absurdly formulated but crucial 'philosophical' question in the form of a résumé of the misadventures related in the *conte:*

> Je voudrais savoir lequel est le pire, ou d'être violée cent fois par des pirates nègres, d'avoir une fesse coupée, de passer par les baguettes chez les Bulgares, d'être fouetté et pendu dans un auto-da-fé, d'être disséqué, de ramer en galère, d'éprouver enfin toutes les misères par lesquelles nous avons tous passé, ou bien de rester ici à ne rien faire.[4]

One of the distinctive features of twentieth-century fiction is the expansion of the roles of the *personnages-embrayeurs* and the *personnages-anaphores*, often at the expense of the *personnage-référentiel*. Such historical, mythological, allegorical or stereotypical characters as are included in twentieth-century fiction tend to be treated in ways which subvert or parody their universal cultural currency. Thus in his highly sardonic novel *L'Invitation*, Claude Simon refuses to name the world-famous. Arthur Miller is referred to as 'l'Américain' who 'n'était pas seulement le second mari de la plus belle fille du monde, avait aussi écrit des pièces à succès sur des sujets à succès comme par exemple le suicide—certains disent: l'assassinat par des services secrets—de la poupée de chair aux adorables épaules, aux seins comme des fruits, à la voix enrouée de bébé'.[5] Similarly, Gorbachev and Reagan are described in readily identifiable terms, but not named:

> le visage que depuis un peu plus d'un an des millions de postes de télévision et des milliers de photographies avaient déjà rendu familier au monde entier: jeune encore, rond, aux traits fins, au regard intelligent [,...] l'air, avec sa calvitie, son sobre veston bleu marine et sa cravate de bon goût du dernier rejeton d'une lignée de gangsters. (pp. 38-9)

> l'autre chef d'État qui pouvait aussi, d'un mot, détruire une bonne moitié de la terre: un acteur encore, un homme qui avait accédé à cette fonction non en vertu de capacités ou de connaissances spéciales mais à force de galoper sur un cheval, coiffé d'un chapeau de cow-boy et souriant de toutes ses dents, dans des films de troisième catégorie. (p. 13)

Alain Robbe-Grillet's novel *Les Gommes* (1953) weaves a network of Oedipal allusions around the central character, but the unwary reader

---

[4] *Candide*, ed. J.H. Brumfitt (Oxford: O.U.P., 1968), p. 147.

[5] *L'Invitation* (Paris: Éditions de Minuit, 1987), p. 65.

who would see in Wallas a classic Oedipal case, i.e. an identifiable psychological type, will simply have fallen into Robbe-Grillet's elaborate interpretive trap.

In contradistinction, the *personnages-anaphores* and *personnages-embrayeurs* enjoy a particular prominence in twentieth-century fiction. With the recognition of the relativity of all narrative accounts, the anaphoric character came into his own; reality was seen to be the sum of the multitude of conflicting perspectives on it and narratorial control was handed over to a multitude of characters whose memories and confidences relativised and contradicted each other. Gide's *Faux-monnayeurs* is full of such internal narrators, whose confusion and misinformation are apparent only to the reader. *Les Faux-monnayeurs* also includes in Édouard an example of a character-type which anticipates the more recent preoccupations of the *nouveau roman*. Édouard, the aspiring novelist and diarist, foreshadows the narrator and the central character of Michel Butor's *L'Emploi du temps* (1956). In this novel, Revel—who is both a *personnage-embrayeur* and a *personnage-anaphore* —embarks upon the apparently banal task of keeping a diary of a year in his life. However, since he only begins his diary five months into that year, he is forced at one and the same time both to record the distant and immediate past and constantly to revise his record in the light of ever-proliferating new data. The sheer volume of his material, his confusion, his exhaustion, and the time-limit which he has set himself preclude definitive success, but he establishes within his text a complex and fascinating network of internal cross-reference. Ultimately, his incomplete account stands as a testimony to the impossible but constructive task with which any writer is faced.

Hamon's classification of characters into three broad categories is only the first step in his exploration of the character as a sign in a textual system. Like the linguistic sign, the character is represented by a discontinuous signifier, that is to say by a set of *marques* which are distributed at varying intervals in the course of the narrative and which Hamon calls the *étiquette*. In the third-person narrative, the coordinates around which these *marques* revolve is the proper name. The coherence of the text and its naturalisation depend to a large extent upon the recurrence and stability of the name: in most straightforward third-person narratives the name of the character will remain the same throughout the text, and if it changes, the change will be explained by a development in the plot such as marriage, divorce, the adoption of an alias or a pen name, etc. As the text advances, the *étiquette* is normally reduced for the sake of economy. Typically, in the nineteenth-century realist or naturalist novel, the physical and psychological description attached to the proper name on the appearance of the character gives way to the proper name only, and although the proper name appears at regular intervals, it is frequently replaced by pronouns and other substitutes. In the establishment of the *étiquette*, the novelist may, for clarity, go as far as to introduce family trees. However, the function of the *étiquette* is not purely elucidative or economical. As Hamon points out, the *étiquette* can also serve a thematic function. Variations in the use of the name or substitutes may act as an indication of the narrator's attitude towards the character, or may be used to highlight a particular thematic dimension associated with him. A survey of the many periphrastic epithets applied to Lucien in Balzac's *Illusions perdues* reveals the many conflicting roles assumed by him in his attempt to rise in society, together with the narrator's ironic attitude towards him or distaste for him on certain occasions.[6] Thus, Lucien is variously dubbed 'le poète', 'le jeune homme' (p. 56), 'l'amant' (p. 58), 'le Byron d'Angoulême', 'le grand homme d'Angoulême' (p. 135), 'l'enfant noble et pur' (p. 153), 'pauvre amoureux' (p. 175), 'le grand homme de province' (pp. 187, 233, 301, 308, 529), 'le poète furieux' (p. 197), 'le néophyte' (pp. 279, 350, 371), 'le poète de province' (pp. 299, 306), 'le poète des *Marguerites*' (p. 366), 'l'ami du Cénacle' (p. 367), 'le pauvre grand homme de province' (p. 537).

In *Illusions perdues,* the epithet acts as a marker by which to chart Lucien's rise and fall, the extent of his self-destruction and the narrator's attitude towards him. The epithet serves a rather different function in *Exercices de style,* in which Raymond Queneau offers ninety-nine versions of a banal dispute on a bus.[7] With virtually every new version the *étiquette* is expanded, each new epithet contributing another dimension to the multi-facetted portrait: 'un poulet au grand cou' (p. 11); 'un ridicule jouvenceau' (p. 15); 'le foutriquet' (p. 18); 'un morveux' (p. 25); 'un longicol tresseautourduchapeauté morveux' (p. 28); 'une ridicule éphèbe' (p. 39); 'un zozo l'air pied' (p. 64); 'un quidam' (p. 73). The sheer range of the epithets which include the insulting, the obscene, the fanciful, the neologistic, and the archaic is a source of humour, an indication of the subjectivity of any account, and a display of verbal gymnastics. More recent experimental fiction also frequently debunks the traditional economical function of the *étiquette*. In Robbe-Grillet's novel *Projet pour une révolution à New York* (1970), this is transferable. Characters have no stable physical features, don a variety of masks, and several characters share names.

As with the linguistic sign, so in the case of the character-sign, the relationship between the signifier and the signified is by definition arbitrary. However, while recognising this fundamental arbitrariness, it is nevertheless important to analyse the extent to which it is motivated by the author or the narrator. Hamon identifies various procedures by which writers attempt to naturalise the name:

---

[6] The following page references relate to the the 1961 Garnier Frères edition.

[7] The following page references relate to the Gallimard 'Folio' edition (1947).

1. *Visual indications.* The writer may exploit the diagrammatic
possibilities of language, attributing a name beginning with an O to a fat
character, a name beginning with an I to a thin character. On a slightly
more sophisticated level, the length and number of syllables used in the
name may be an indication of the character's social status, while the
order in which characters are introduced in a sentence may intimate
their relative importance in the narrative.

2. *Acoustic indications.* The sound of a name may relate to aspects
of a character's personality, the features of a place or to the attitude of
the author or narrator towards him or it. In *Candide,* as Sherman points
out, 'the name Thunder-ten-tronckh [...] mocks what the French heard
as plosive and heavy in Prussian names of place and of families'.[8]

3. *Morphological and logical elements.* The treatment of proper
names as though they were ordinary words, and the production of
names using prefixes, suffixes, articles and prepositions, may serve to
refer to a particular social, moral or ideological context. The name
which is etymologically related to or derived from other words retains
some of the connotations of the original. Voltaire's Candide is indeed a
candid character, while Pangloss, whose name is derived from the
Greek 'pan glossa' ('all tongue') is verbally unstoppable. In the same
work, Pococurante is given a name which reflects his personality;
'"Poco curante", in Italian, means "caring little", and is thus a very
appropriate name for the disenchanted individual Voltaire describes'.[9]
Flaubert's Bovary and Bouvard are both bovine in name and in nature.

4. *Intertextual reference.* In the great serial novels of the nineteenth
century, and in particular in Zola, the surname of a character may refer
the reader back to a family history which to a significant degree will
determine the character's behaviour:

> [Le nom de famile est] la marque explicite de la présence d'une hérédité (la
> persistance du même) à travers une diversité et une pluralité. Par là, il
> rattache le personnage à une origine (tante Dide pour les Rougon-Macquart),
> donc à un destin (la menace permanente d'une catastrophe)...[10]

The degree of motivation of a name is one measure of the *lisibilité* of
the text, since the clearly and fully motivated name sums up a multitude
of relevant information that will explain the behaviour and actions of
the character. However, the motivation of the name is not a guarantee of
knowledge or truth. As Hamon points out, a character whose name

---

[8] Carol Sherman, *Reading Voltaire's 'Contes': A Semiotics of Philosophical Narration* (Chapel
Hill: N. Carolina Studies in the Romance Languages and Literatures, 1985), p. 141.

[9] Brumfitt, *op. cit.,* p. 185.

[10] Hamon, *Le Personnel du roman,* p. 108.

signifies purity may have an evil personality which is only revealed at a
later stage in the narrative. The attribution of a name to a character may
also be determined by a spirit of contradiction on the part of the author,
or by a desire to provoke interpretive speculation in the reader:

> Appeler une grosse dame 'la mère Fétu' (*Une page d'amour*), ou appeler
> quelqu'un de perpétuellement triste 'Dejoie' (*L'Argent*), c'est poser au
> lecteur un problème d'interprétation. L'antiphrase, semble-t-il, stimule
> davantage l'activité herméneutique du lecteur que la motivation
> concordante.[11]

The signifier or name may itself be of central thematic interest in
works which, for example, centre on the search for a personal identity,
the identification of origins, or the revelation of the unknown. Hamon
gives the examples of the attempt to name the unnameable in fantasy
literature and the demasking of characters with pseudonyms in the
detective novel. Social considerations may ensure that the name is a
central preoccupation of one of the characters. Thus, in *Illusions
perdues*, Lucien Chardon adopts his mother's aristocratic name as an aid
in his attempt to climb the social ladder, while his self-effacing mother,
who through penury becomes a midwife, takes the name Madame
Charlotte to avoid shaming her ambitious son.

Hamon opens his discussion of the signified of the character-sign
with a barrage of quotations from other theorists that constitute the
premises of his own argument:

> Un personnage de roman naît seulement des unités de sens, n'est fait que de
> phrases prononcées par lui ou sur lui. (Wellek and Warren)

> [Le personnage] est un 'assemblage de traits différentiels [,...] de traits
> distinctifs'. (Lotman)

> Les acteurs sont des lexèmes [...] qui se trouvent organisés, à l'aide de
> relations syntaxiques, en énoncés univoques. (Greimas)

> Le personnage est comparable à un mot rencontré dans un document, mais
> qui ne figure pas au dictionnaire, ou encore à un nom propre, c'est-à-dire à
> un terme dépourvu de contexte.(Lévi-Strauss)[12]

For Hamon, as for the theorists whom he cites, the character is
essentially a construction put together in the course of a reading, which
therefore depends heavily on the rememorative and correlating
competence of the reader.
    Frequently, that rememorative competence will necessarily extend
beyond the limits of the text and encompass the larger intertext of

---

[11] *Ibid.*, p. 128.

[12] 'Pour un statut sémiologique du personnage', pp. 125-6, and notes, pp. 170-71.

history and culture, since the roles played by historical or mythological characters are predetermined. In the nineteenth-century serial novel, the character is intertextually pre-programmed by hereditary factors. Hamon points out that Nana, as the daughter of Gervaise and Coupeau and as a Macquart, is destined for disaster.

By contrast, fiction which does not incorporate such specific intertextual references gradually and progressively constructs around the proper name a composite signified. The name, an empty signifier at the outset, accumulates meaning in the course of the narrative by means of portraits, leitmotifs, etc. However, accumulation is only part of the process. Opposition and differentiation establish distinctions among the characters and among characteristics within the character. The reader, Hamon insists, must therefore attempt to analyse and classify characters according to the information made available in the narrative. The establishment of the relevant differential axes for a given work is a prerequisite for the successful classification of character. Hamon's own choice of axes—sexuality, geographical origin, ideology and financial position—applies in particular to the naturalist novel and, clearly, must be adapted and refined to accommodate the dominant ideological or aesthetic characteristics of other periods. The next step in this process of differential analysis is the tabulation of the characters and the information offered about them.

	Sexuality	Geographical origin	Ideology	Financial position
C 1	+	+		+
C 2	+		+	+
C 3		+		
C 4			+	+

The more information we have about a character, the more
important he or she is likely to be. Thus, characters 1 and 2 are likely to
be more important than the other characters (e.g. hero and heroine,
principal adversaries, etc.) The tabulation of information may also
suggest certain pairings or contrasts. The information about the sexual
attractions/inclinations of characters 1 and 2 may indicate a liaison
between them, while the fact that characters 2 and 4 both register
positively in the columns relating to ideology and financial position may
suggest a compatibility which threatens the relationship between
characters 1 and 2.

An initial, crude tabulation allows the analyst to group characters
into broad classes. Having established broad categories, the analyst must
try to elaborate a graduational scale which will allow him to identify
dominant characters/characteristics and to shed light on the more
indeterminate character or characteristic. Qualifications of character
and references to behaviour or potential behaviour should be analysed
in relation to their quantity (single or repeated) and their formulation
(implicit or explicit). Thus, the character/characteristic who/which is
mentioned explicitly and repeatedly is likely to be more important than
one who/which is alluded to only once or implicitly.

The analysis of the functions of characters within a given text
demands of the reader a methodological approach which seeks to
identify 'le modèle actantiel qui organise chaque séquence' (p. 138).
Hamon, like Greimas, distinguishes between the *acteurs* or
personnages, as they are defined by portraits, qualifications, etc., and
the *actants,* or archetypal functions of narrative grammar. The actantial
approach to narrative compares the structure of plot with sentence
structure. As Jonathan Culler explains, it is:

> essentially a process of reducing the sentences to a series of subjects and
> predicates which will be cast in a constant form so that they can be related to
> one another and, as it were, added up. Everything referring to the act of
> enunciation is first eliminated: first and second person pronouns [...], all
> references to the time of the message, deictics, in so far as they are
> dependent on the situation of the speaker and not simply on other parts of
> the message [...]. Each sequence is then reduced to a set of nominal phrases
> (*actants*) and a predicate which is either a verb or predicative adjective [...].
> *Actants* or nominal groups will fit into one of six different roles: subject,
> object, *destinateur* (sender), *destinataire* (receiver), *opposant* (opponent)
> and *adjuvant* (helper). (*SP,* pp. 81-2)

In determining the function of a particular set of characters within a
plot, a sub-plot or a narrative sequence, the reader focuses upon the
deep structure of the narrative, the paradigmatic roles occupied by
characters, and the ways in which the *actant* relates to other *actants* in a
given plot, sub-plot or sequence. A narrative's conformity, or not, to
this model is an indicator of the degree of *lisibilité* of a text:

> La non-perturbation de cette structure est donc un élément important de sa
> lisibilité, lisibilité liée au fait que le lecteur peut non seulement *situer* un
> personnage dans une échelle de personnages-types et de relations
> d'oppositions ou de ressemblances, mais aussi *prévoir* certains
> déroulements-types.[13]

Such a model works particularly well in the analysis of folk-tales and
stories involving quests, ordeals, contracts and conspiracy, where the
subject will, in his pursuit of a particular object encounter opponents
and helpers and possibly givers and receivers. Thus, Carol Sherman
identifies three quests in *Candide*—the marriage quest, the quest for
freedom and the quest for the fusion of theory and experience—and for
each of these quests she has produced a tabulation indicating the actantial
roles taken by characters or other elements of the narrative.[14]

Valery Larbaud's short story *L'Heure avec la figure*,[15] which draws
heavily upon the fairy tale and the adventure story, can be translated
into the following actantial schema:

Subject: 'un petit garçon'

Object: 'six heures'

Adversaire: 'l'ennui', i.e. 'Monsieur Marcatte et son solfège',
                 and 'une heure libre [,...] mais vide, sans jeu'.

Adjuvant: 'la Figure dans les veines du marbre de la cheminée'.

Furthermore, in his quest to find something to combat boredom, the
little boy also becomes the receiver of material for the fabrication of his
time-passing fantasy. The donor is his physical surroundings, described
at the beginning of the tale, which give him a set of sensory data and
images ('rayon', 'sentinelle', 'roses', 'bleu', 'ombres', 'meubles') on
which to build his imaginary adventure story.

Hamon's argument that the character is in part defined by his
capacity to be categorised within a particular class of *actants* is borne
out by works which have strongly articulated plots or which are based
upon archetypal narrative structures. A more general application
remains a problem. As Culler points out, 'it seems likely that anyone
using the model to study a variety of stories will need to exercise
considerable ingenuity in discovering appropriate senders and receivers'
(*SP*, p. 234). The plots and sub-plots of Balzac and Zola lend themselves
fairly readily to actantial analysis, partly because of the strength of the

---

[13] 'Pour un statut sémiologique du personnage', p. 140

[14] *Reading Voltaire's 'Contes'*, pp. 165-89.

[15] *Enfantines* (Paris: Gallimard, 1950).

story line and party because of a relatively naive approach to point of view. Much modern fiction resists the identification of actantial roles, either because of the looseness of plot construction or because the production and interpretation of significance are centred upon the teller rather than the tale.

The final section of Hamon's essay draws together some of the threads of his argument and confronts the problems surrounding the concept of the 'hero', which is one of the most ill-defined terms of literary criticism. The identification of the protagonist or hero of a work is normally a relatively unproblematic activity. However, an understanding of the ways in which a protagonist is signalled, of the ways in which he or she is distinguished from other characters, and of the relationship between the hero and the prevalent cultural code not only permits the establishment of a hierarchy of characters, but also sheds light upon the evolution and revision to which the notion of 'hero' is subject. Hamon's suggested model is based on the differential procedures employed in texts to designate the hero:

1. *Differential qualification.* The character is the peg on which a certain number of qualifications are hung, qualifications which differentiate him from other characters either because they do not have particular attributes or have them to a lesser degree, e.g.:

genealogy mentioned	no reference to genealogy
surname, forename, nickname provided	anonymous
physical description	no physical description
psychologically motivated	no psychological motivation
character is both participant and narrator	character is participant only
character involved in romantic relationship with another central character	no romantic relationship
character is: handsome strong noble	ugly weak commoner, etc.

2. *Differential distribution* (i.e. quantitative differentiation)

Does he/she appear:

at crucial moments, turning-points	only at transitional, unmarked moments
frequently	infrequently, episodically, only once

3. *Differentiation on the basis of a character's autonomy or lack of autonomy.*

Hamon suggests that the hero appears alone or combined with an assortment of characters according to the context, whereas other characters may appear in pairs. The reader must determine whether or not a character is 'tied' to another one, and how much freedom of movement a particular character enjoys. The reader should also establish whether or not a character is given both monologues and dialogues. If he or she is confined to dialogues, he/she is more likely to be a secondary character.

4. *Differentiation on the basis of function.* How much does the character contribute to the action of the narrative? Hamon suggests certain crucial oppositions:

mediating character (i.e. resolves contradictions)	not a mediating character
defined by what he does	defined by what he says or what is said about him
has an opponent whom he defeats	fails to defeat his opponent
receives information, has knowledge	doesn't receive information doesn't have knowledge
realises himself, i.e. realises projects, comes to an understanding of himself	doesn't realise himself
has helpers	doesn't have helpers

| is a participant in an initial contract which gives him a goal, achieved by the end of the story | doesn't take part in a contract |
| makes good an initial deficiency | doesn't make good an initial deficiency |

5. *A conventional predesignation* (i.e. the genre defines the hero *a priori*). Genre may act as a common code between reader and author and restrict and predetermine the reader's expectations.

6. *Explicit commentary.* The reader is told who is the hero and who is the traitor, who is good, bad, wise, stupid, normal, abnormal, etc. Thus the reader may encounter commentaries on:

a) the language of the character, his facility with words, the reliability of his statements.

b) the technical skills of the character, his competence in certain domains.

c) the character's ability to interact socially, the appropriateness of his behaviour in certain contexts.

One must, of course, treat such markers with care. The central theme of the text may be the contradiction between appearance and reality. The character's good deeds may be a way of covering evil motives; his confidence may mask a lack of competence; his inappropriate behaviour may have deep-rooted and honourable causes.

7. *Redundancy.* The central character is overdetermined by multiple emphatic devices. The privilege of his position is marked by redundancy, a superabundance of pointers:

The use of décor to mirror the character.

The use of metaphor and image to accentuate the character.

The use of helpers and allies who reflect one of the characteristics of the hero.

The use of allusion (e.g. mythological, historical, literary, etc.) to predetermine his destiny.

The reference to repeated actions which define the character as belonging to a certain class.

Problems relating to the status of the protagonist (hero, anti-hero, villain) can be resolved to some extent by a consideration of the selective restrictions at work within a given narrative code. The sign, Hamon points out, is defined in part by selective restrictions or rules which limit its possibilities of combination with other signs. These rules are varied in nature and may be linguistic, logical, aesthetic, or ideological. The analysis of the character in relation to the aesthetic rules pertaining to the genre and to the values and moral norms of a culture will normally facilitate identification of the hero. Thus the hero of the medieval romance will be a knight, while the hero of a social realist novel will normally be a worker.

The text which, in its conformity with contemporary *bienséances* and moral values, tends towards the *lisible* will be characterised by a coincidence between the values of the hero and the norms of the period. These norms will vary historically and culturally. Therefore, in reading the works of other cultures or periods, one must understand and take into account the values of that culture or period. Of course, the text may well set out to disrupt or question prevailing moral or ideological codes. In such cases, the hero is generally a more problematical figure. Thus, in *L'Étranger*, Meursault's behaviour in the first part of the novel will shock and alienate the average reader. Meursault's perspective is valorised not by his conformity to the norms of his (or our) culture, but by his differentiation from other members of society. Meursault's apparent callousness may be difficult to condone, but society's self-righteousness and hypocrisy are ultimately much more abhorrent.

Sexuality is clearly a key factor in assessing the character's status and his/her conformity to social mores. Hamon borrows Greimas's modelling of the permissible and the taboo in sexual matters:

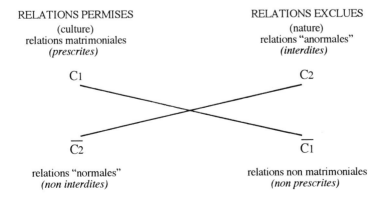

RELATIONS PERMISES   RELATIONS EXCLUES
(culture)   (nature)
relations matrimoniales   relations "anormales"
(prescrites)   *(interdites)*

C_1 C_2

$\overline{C_2}$ $\overline{C_1}$

relations "normales"   relations non matrimoniales
(non interdites)   *(non prescrites)*

On aura par exemple:

C1 : amours conjugales.

C2 : inceste, homosexualité.

$\overline{C2}$: adultère de l'homme.

$\overline{C1}$: adultère de la femme.[16]

In many societies the poles *C1* and *C2* have been privileged. Conjugal love and adultery by the man do not generally run counter to social expectations; by contrast, relationships which deviate from the norm (incest, bestiality, homosexuality and adultery by women) do infringe the moral and religious codes of many societies. The text which simply seeks to reinforce prevailing codes will condone male adultery but condemn female adultery. Texts which question society's assumptions and prejudices will, of course, valorise different character-types. The feminist novels of Monique Wittig promote the lesbian relationship, while Constant's *Adolphe* exposes the double standards of a society which colludes with exploitative male sexuality and severely censures its female victims. In *Zazie dans le métro*, Raymond Queneau subverts taboo after taboo as he introduces a motley gallery of characters whose sexual diversity shows humanity at its most imaginative.

*****

It is unlikely that many readers or critics will be tempted to apply Philippe Hamon's taxonomical method as rigorously as he does in his own study on Zola. There is no doubt that his approach is excessively painstaking and slow for the average reader, and at times it may seem that he is suggesting a rather circuitous route in order to establish the obvious. However, in analysing fictional procedures which many of us take for granted, Hamon forces us to review our humanist assumptions about character, and elucidates the multiple textual processes by which a fictional character is constructed. If a comprehensive and exhaustive application of his differential and actantial models remains beyond the tolerance of most readers, his identification and inventory of the standard devices of characterisation in the nineteenth-century novel offers a serviceable coordinate by which to measure the *lisibilité* of a text.

---

[16] 'Pour un statut sémiologique du personnage', p. 152, derived from A.J. Greimas, *Du sens* (Paris: Seuil, 1970), p. 142.

Exercises

1. Discuss the ways in which play on the *étiquette* contributes to the comedy in Queneau's *Zazie dans le métro.*

2. Comment on the ways in which the writer subverts the conventional use of the *étiquette* in one of the following:

   (a) Nathalie Sarraute's *Martereau.*

   (b) Alain Robbe-Grillet's *Projet pour une révolution à New York.*

3. What is the effect of the delay in naming the narrator in Camus's *La Peste* ?

4. Read chapter one of *Illusions perdues* and try to identify the differential devices used in the characterisation of Lucien Chardon and David Séchard.

5. Camus's Meursault is not a hero in the conventional sense in that he does not conform to contemporary social mores. To what extent does Hamon's theory help one define more precisely Meursault's heroic status?

6. To what extent do Hamon's comments on sexuality and characterisation help one analyse Michel in *L'Immoraliste* ?

Chapter Four

Narrative Order, Frequency and Speed

Gérard Genette's critical and theoretical work is wide-ranging. *Figures I* and *Figures II* [1] are collections of essays that offer new approaches to numerous, apparently critically exhausted works, while his monumental *Palimpsestes* has taken him into the field of 'hypertextualité' or 'littérature [...] qui s'écrit en lisant'.[2] However, he is perhaps best known for his highly influential analysis of the relationships between story-time and discourse-time. 'Discours du récit', which forms the major part of *Figures III,* [3] offers both a painstaking analysis of the temporal relationships in Proust's *A la recherche du temps perdu* and a critical model which can in principle be applied to any work of fiction. Genette's argument centres upon the discrepancies between the order, frequency, and duration of events in the fictional world and the order, frequency, and duration of their narration. In focusing upon these discrepancies, Genette exposes the extent to which time is manipulated and restructured in narrative discourse. The identification of such discrepancies is clearly a key to interpretation. Not only does it allow the reader to distinguish more clearly the turning-points of the plot, but it also provides crucial indications about narratorial priorities, assumptions, intentions, and reliability.

Order of narration

The analysis commences with a quotation from Metz's seminal work on the cinema that sums up the problem to be addressed in fiction:

> Le récit est une séquence deux fois temporelle [...]: il y a le temps de la chose-racontée et le temps du récit (temps du signifié et temps du signifiant). Cette dualité n'est pas seulement ce qui rend possibles toutes les distorsions temporelles qu'il est banal de relever dans les récits (trois ans de la vie du heros résumés en deux phrases d'un roman, ou en quelques plans d'un montage 'fréquentatif' de cinéma, etc.); plus fondamentalement, elle nous invite à constater que l'une des fonctions du récit est de monnayer un temps dans un autre temps.[4]

---

[1] Paris: Seuil, 1966 and 1969, respectively.

[2] Paris: Seuil, 1982.

[3] Paris: Seuil, 1972. Henceforth, 'Discours du récit' will be referred to as *DR*.

[4] C. Metz, *Essais sur la signification au cinéma* (Klincksieck, 1968), p. 27, quoted in *DR*, p. 77.

Genette goes on to argue that, while there would seem to be a correlation between the chronology of the story and the order of narration in the folk tale, in Western literary tradition there are considerable disparities between the two.[5] The *récit*, or account, is generally littered with *anachronies*, a term which he applies to the 'différentes formes de discordance entre l'ordre de l'histoire et celui du récit' (*DR*, p. 79). Such *anachronies* are constants in the Western *récit*, from the Greek epic to the modern novel. Genette cites as an example the first four hundred or so lines of the *Iliad*, where after a few lines in which the quarrel between Achilles and Agamemnon is evoked, the narrative launches into a long retrospective explanation.

While the expository retrospection is a very familiar and readily identifiable narrative device, Genette's study of Proustian manipulation of chronological order in *A la recherche du temps perdu* shows that the *anachronie* affects not only the macrostructure of the fictional work and the ordering of substantial narrative segments and sequences, but also the microstructure and the relationships between sentences and clauses. As Diana Knight points out:

> To follow through Genette's analysis is to become very aware of the astonishing zigzagging in time at the microcosmic level of Proust's novel, even at points where the main story-line unfolds in a more or less linear manner. [...] Despite all the critical ink spilled over Proust's philosophy of time and memory, this basic yet rather extraordinary feature of the narrative organisation of time seems simply not to have been noticed. To read Proust after Genette is necessarily to read with a constant awareness of the novel's narrative 'game with time', a game which according to Genette, perhaps subsumes its better-known themes of time.[6]

Anachronies divide into two basic categories—the *prolepse* and the *analepse*. The *prolepse* corresponds roughly to the cinemato-graphic notion of 'flashforward', while the *analepse* corresponds to the notion of 'flashback'. However, Genette's terms, if a little rebarbative, are preferable to their cinematographic counterparts in that they are psychologically neutral and allow the reader to analyse the temporal organisation of the text independently of psychological assumptions. This independence is particularly important in the study of self-reflexive fiction, where the *anachronie* frequently serves a purely disruptive, formal function and cannot be naturalised psychologically.

The *anachronie* offers access to the past or future of the story and constitutes a secondary récit within the main account:

> Toute anachronie constitue par rapport au récit dans lequel elle s'insère—sur lequel elle se greffe—un récit temporellement second. (*DR*, p. 90)

---

[5] Compare Michel Butor, *Essais sur le roman* (Paris: Gallimard, 1969), pp. 109-124.

[6] 'Joseph Conrad, *Heart of Darkness*', in Tallack, *Literary Theory at Work*, p. 13.

Thus, a given sequence of events in real time (1 2 3) may be recounted in an order which incorporates an *analepse* (2 3 1) or a *prolepse* (3 1 2). Michael Toolan explains the effect of the two types of *anachronies* from the point of view of the reader:

> Any delayed disclosure (the reader expected, on the basis of chronological sequences, to be told this earlier) is thus analeptic, while any premature disclosure (the reader did not expect, if strict chronology were observed, to be told this until later) is proleptic.[7]

Obviously, given the predominantly retrospective tendency of the activity of storytelling, the *analepse* is the more common type of *anachronie*. Its most obvious function is to provide additional information relating to the background of a character or an event. The opening chapters of many novels incorporate substantial *analepses* which provide summary histories of a character's early life or development or the events preceding and leading to a particular situation. Thus, in Gide's *L'Immoraliste*, Michel's account of his own family history[8] lays the ground for his subsequent development and rebellion against his past, while at the same time highlighting personal features— obsessiveness, an ignorance of other people and in particular of the opposite sex—which are to determine much of his future behaviour. In Balzac's fiction, the history of a particular location may be as important as that of some of the characters. Hence his description of setting may well incorporate multiple brief *analepses* which show the environmental factors contributing to the formation of a character or a social group. The long description of Angoulême in the second chapter of *Illusions perdues* incorporates numerous *analepses* which highlight factors essential to an understanding of Lucien's driving ambition: the economic divide separating the inhabitants of the 'ville haute' and l'Houmeau; the decline of the town and its increasing provincialism; the high quality of its educational system; and its inveterate caste mentality.

The introduction of a new character or narrative sequence is also frequently the cue for an *analepse:*

> Tout personnage nouveau, à y regarder d'un peu plus près, amène des explications sur son passé, un retour en arrière, et bientôt ce qui sera essentiel pour comprendre le récit, ce ne sera pas seulement le passé de tel ou tel, mais ce que les autres en connaissent ou ignorent à tel moment.[9]

The amplitude of such *analepses* will clearly vary according to the importance of the character or the importance attached to the character by the narrator. Thus, in Constant's *Adolphe*, the narrator shows his

---

[7] Toolan, *Narrative: A Critical Linguistic Introduction*, p. 50.

[8] Gallimard, 'Folio' edition, pp. 17-19.

[9] Butor, *op. cit.*, p. 113.

receptiveness to all available information about Ellénore and paints us a picture of past devotion, self-sacrifice and fidelity. By contrast, Baron de T***, the principal spokesman of self-interested society is introduced simply by an epithet referring to his social status: 'J'écris au baron de T***, notre ministre dans le pays ou vous êtes'.[10]

The *prolepse* has traditionally been a much less frequently employed device, largely because of the preference in most fiction for retrospective narration and because of the concern to maintain suspense:

> Le souci de suspense narratif propre à la conception 'classique' du roman (au sens large, et dont le centre de gravité se trouve plutôt au XIXe siècle) s'accommode mal d'une telle pratique, non plus d'ailleurs que la fiction traditionnelle d'un narrateur qui doit sembler découvrir en quelque sorte l'histoire en même temps qu'il la raconte. Aussi trouvera-t-on fort peu de prolepses chez un Balzac, un Dickens ou un Tolstoï. (*DR*, pp. 105-106)

In defining the *prolepse*, Genette is careful to distinguish it from other prospective features such as omens, clues, etc. These latter devices, which he calls *amorces,* are suggestive rather than informative and do not radically disrupt the chronology of events. Their function in the text is recognised retrospectively and their effect depends much more upon readerly competence:

> A la différence de l'annonce, l'amorce n'est donc en principe, à sa place dans le texte, qu'un 'germe insignifiant', et même imperceptible, dont la valeur de germe ne sera reconnue que plus tard, et de façon rétrospective. Encore faut-il tenir compte de l'éventuelle (ou plutôt variable) *compétence* narrative du lecteur, née de l'habitude, qui permet de déchiffrer de plus en plus vite le code narratif en général, ou propre à tel genre ou à telle œuvre, et d'identifier les 'germes' dès leur apparition. (*DR*, p. 113)

The *prolepse,* however, effects a real reversal in the ordering of events. In fiction which aims to be naturalistic and which therefore disguises manipulative devices, the *prolepse* is found most commonly in works employing a first-person narrator, who in telling his own story may legitimately allude to subsequent events and establish connections between different parts of his tale:

> Le récit 'à la première personne' se prête mieux qu'aucun autre à l'anticipation, du fait même de son caractère rétrospectif déclaré qui autorise le narrateur à des allusions à l'avenir, et particulièrement à sa situation présente, qui font en quelque sorte partie de son rôle. (*DR*, p. 106)

In character- or plot-centred fiction the function of the *analepse* is then generally informative and economical; it is a convenient means of giving the reader immediate access to essential and explanatory data relating to a character or set of circumstances. In the case of much

---

[10] Le Livre de Poche (1972), p. 92.

modern fiction, for instance the *nouveau roman*, which is primarily concerned with exploring the question of representation itself, the *analepse* may serve a parodical function. In Robbe-Grillet's *Le Voyeur* (1955), the repeated references to Mathias's penchant for collecting string as a child act as an unreliable and facetious clue to the unwary reader, who may be tempted to relate it to the suggestions of a bondage obsession elsewhere in the text. However, these suggestions are nowhere confirmed by the text and remain as tenuous as those relating to Mathias's 'murder' of Jacqueline/Violette. In Michel Butor's *L'Emploi du temps*, the *analepse* likewise serves to confuse rather than to clarify. Here, the narrator's attempt to write a recapitulative diary which will at once record the present and allow him to catch up on the previous five months of his stay in England is doomed to failure. Not only does the volume of data from those earlier months constantly threaten his chronicling of the present, but new information requires a perpetual revision of the past. Whereas in more traditional fiction, the *analepse* provided the reader with reliable coordinates in the past, in the *nouveau roman* it destabilises the 'story', indicates the incalculable quantity of factors contributing to a particular situation, and the impossibility of establishing a clear chronological or logical chain of events.

The function of the *prolepse* varies according to the priorities of the text. It may, for example, contribute to the development of irony or a sense of tragedy, in that it gives the reader access to knowledge denied to some or all of the characters. In *L'Immoraliste,* the prefatory letter from the friend to whom Michel has confided his story, and in particular the narrator's remarks about the effect Michel's story has had on him, cast an ominous irony over Michel's lyrical and enthusiastic commentaries on his experiences at certain points in the narrative.

Paradoxically, the *prolepse* may also contribute to the production of suspense. Linear revelation of cause and effect may be abandoned and replaced by an exploration of the many factors which combine to produce a particular outcome. In such fiction the suspense is not dependent upon the reader's speculation about the outcome; rather it hinges upon the reader's desire to understand how a particular outcome or situation could arise in the first place. As Michael Toolan points out:

> Prolepses [...] undercut or remove suspense, since they reveal future circumstances to you long before any chronological imperative dictates that they be told. On the other hand, a different kind of engaged puzzlement is fostered by prolepses: the reader is frequently made aware of her own bafflement as to how characters and events get from their current situation to the distant future one prematurely revealed, and is all the more intrigued to learn of the intervening happenings. (p. 53)

Thus, the third paragraph of Maupassant's story *Qui sait?* offers us

information about the narrator's present state, and this whets our desire
to know more about the circumstances or events which have caused the
breakdown of his health:

> Je suis aujourd'hui dans une maison de santé; mais j'y suis entré
> volontairement, par prudence, par peur! Un seul être connaît mon histoire.
> Le médecin d'ici. Je vais l'écrire. Je ne sais trop pourquoi? Pour m'en
> débarrasser, car je la sens en moi comme un intolérable cauchemar.[11]

In *Les Fous de Bassan* (1982) by the French-Canadian writer Anne
Hébert, the 'main event'—the disappearance of the Atkins girls—is
recounted in the first section, and the rest of the narrative consists of a
reconstruction from many different points of view of the events
preceding their disappearance.

Frequency

Genette's term 'fréquence narrative' refers to the relationship
between the number of times an event takes place in the story and the
number of times it is actually narrated. He divides the types of narrative
frequency into three broad categories: *récit singulatif*, *récit répétitif*,
and *récit itératif*. The *récit singulatif* applies in cases where what
happens *once* is also narrated *once*. It is the most common type of
narrative frequency, tending as it does to stress narrative progression
and the discreteness of the 'event'. The *récit singulatif* promotes variety
in plot construction and emphasises the uniqueness of a situation, the
vicissitudes of life. Thus, in *Candide*, the characters are exposed to an
inconceivable sequence of dangers, mishaps and adventures each of
which happens once and is, usually, recounted once. In realist fiction,
for instance in novels centred upon the rise and fall of a specific
character or family, or in the *Bildungsroman* or apprenticeship novel,
the *récit singulatif* allows the narrator to focus upon the inexorable
impulse towards an inevitable outcome or to mark the stages of a
character's development. In the work of Georges Bernanos, by contrast,
the predominance of the *récit singulatif* is, as E. Lagadec-Sadoulet
points out, the narrative correlative of his fascination for the
extraordinary and the exceptional:

> A 'l'ivresse de l'itération' que Gérard Genette découvre chez Proust répond
> l'ivresse bernanosienne de la 'singulation'. Les composantes du récit,
> personnages, événements de l'histoire, sont marquées du sceau de
> 'l'extraordinaire'. [...] .A personnages 'extraordinaires', destinées tout
> aussi 'extraordinaires'. [...] Le destin des héros bernanosiens s'inscrit dans

---

[11] *'Le Horla' et autres contes cruels et fantastiques*, ed. M.-C. Bancquart (Paris: Garnier Frères,
1976), p. 511.

une totale nouveauté [...] Car l'instant vécu a tout le poids d'un moment unique. [...] La prédominance du récit singulatif répond donc à une tendance fondamentale du style narratif de Bernanos. Ses romans ne peuvent être qu'une 'suite de tableaux fulgurants'.[12]

Also included under the umbrella term *récit singulatif* is the case where what happens *n* times is recounted *n* times. The author's concern for the tolerance of his reader clearly limits the use of this type of *fréquence*. The hypothetical example which Genette gives would serve as an indication of a fixed monotonous routine which, were it prolonged throughout a novel, would almost certainly frustrate and bore the reader. Used sparingly, however, the *nth* narration of an incident happening *n* times can act as a pointer to intractable habits, recidivism, reflex behaviour etc. Candide's repeated citation of Pangloss is a reminder of his unquestioning reliance upon his mentor and, by its predictability, is an important source of humour. In the first section of *L'Étranger*, Meursault's references to the effects of heat and light upon him on different occasions prepare the reader for his reaction to the Arab on the beach. His susceptibility to heat and light causes him, in normal circumstances, to doze off or, if another character prevents him from doing so, to experience strong feelings of irritation: both reactions which suggest a tendency to abdicate rational responsibility. However, in the scene of the shooting there is no possibility of dozing off. The pressure from the natural elements is greater than in previous scenes and Meursault is in a situation of physical danger which requires action. His initial shot, like his earlier naps and irritation, is a form of self-defence.

Genette's second category of narrative frequency is the *récit répétitif*, where what happens *once* is narrated *n* times. This *fréquence* is particularly favoured by those twentieth-century texts which offer multiple perspectives upon a single event or by self-reflexive texts in which certain 'given' data are combined and recombined to the point of exhaustion. In *La Porte étroite*, Alissa's journal provides an insight into her emotions which sheds cruelly ironic light on her virtuous remarks at her last meeting with Jérôme as they had been recounted by the latter:

Que s'est-il donc passé? Que lui ai-je dit? Qu'ai-je fait? Quel besoin devant lui d'exagérer toujours ma vertu? De quel prix peut être une vertu que mon cœur tout entier renie...[13]

In *Les Fous de Bassan*, the same events—the suicide of Irène, the arrival of Stevens, etc.—are recounted by several different characters, each of whom projects upon them a personal bias. In these novels, the thorny

---

[12] *Temps et récit dans l'œuvre romanesque de Georges Bernanos* (Paris: Klincksieck, 1988), pp. 285-7.

[13] Gallimard, 'Folio' edition (1959), p. 174.

question of responsibility is a central issue. By contrast, the novels of Alain Robbe-Grillet are primarily concerned with exploring the permutational possibilities of language. The repeated account of the killing of the *mille-pieds* in *La Jalousie* (1957) may suggest to us that we are reading the reflections of a pathologically obsessive and potentially violent narrator. However, the absence of firm evidence of a personalised narrator should alert us to the sophisticated game of suggestion through repetition that is being played by Robbe-Grillet.

Genette calls his third category of narrative frequency the *récit itératif*. Here he is concerned with the *single* narration of what has happened *n* times. Traditionally, the *récit itératif* is used to indicate repeated or habitual actions in an economical fashion. Thus at the beginning of *La Peste*, Rieux enumerates the habits and routines of the inhabitants of Oran. It is against this background of stagnation that the dramas of the plague are going to be worked out. In such fiction, the *récit itératif* is conventionally subordinated to the *récit singulatif* and provides a background against which the principal events stand out: 'Comme la description, le récit itératif est, dans le roman traditionnel, *au service* du récit "proprement dit", qui est le récit singulatif' (*DR*, p. 148). Genette argues that Flaubert was the first novelist to grant the *récit singulatif* an independent narrative status:

> Le premier romancier qui ait entrepris de l'émanciper de cette dépendance fonctionnelle est évidemment Flaubert dans *Madame Bovary*, où des pages comme celles qui racontent la vie d'Emma au couvent, à Tostes avant et après le bal à la Vaubyessard, ou ses jeudis à Rouen avec Léon, prennent une amplitude et une autonomie tout à fait inusitées. (*DR*, p. 148)

It is, however, in Proust that Genette detects the best example of what he calls an 'ivresse de l'itératif'. His own survey of the earlier parts of the novel reveals a significant preponderance of iterative accounts:

> Un relevé approximatif [...] fait apparaître quelque chose comme 115 pages itératives contre 70 singulatives dans *Combray*, 91 contre 103 dans *Un Amour de Swann*, 145 contre 113 dans *Gilberte*, soit à peu près 350 contre 285 pour l'ensemble de ces trois sections. Ce n'est qu'à partir du premier séjour à Balbec que s'établit (ou se *rétablit*, si l'on songe à ce qu'était la proportion dans le récit traditionnel) la prédominance du singulatif. (*DR*, p. 149)

Nor is this characteristic to be attributed simply to the Proustian obsession with habit and repetition; it also contributes, by the links which it establishes between discrete events, to the development of the theme of involuntary memory (*DR*, p. 154).

Narrative speed

In his chapter on narrative speed, Genette focuses on the relationship
between the time that an action described takes in the fictional world
and the amount of space devoted to it in the text. In using the term
vitesse narrative, Genette is referring to the relationship between
temporal and spatial measurement, the relationship between the time
covered by a narrative segment (seconds, minutes, hours, weeks, years,
centuries, etc.) and the length of the relevant segments of text (a blank,
a word, a line, a paragraph, a page, *n* pages).

All narrative is, Genette claims, rhythmic; that is to say it
incorporates variations in narrative speed. Genette illustrates his point
by a tabulation of the variations in narrative speed to be found in *A la
recherche du temps perdu.*[14] Thus at one end of the scale, 180 pages can
be devoted to the account of about ten years, while at the other end, 190
pages can be given over to the account of two or three hours.

Theoretically, as Genette points out, there is an infinite gradation of
possible narrative speeds, from ellipsis to descriptive pause:

> Théoriquement, en effet, il existe une gradation continue depuis cette vitesse
> infinie qui est celle de l'ellipse, où un segment nul de récit correspond à une
> durée quelconque d'histoire, jusqu'à cette lenteur absolue qui est celle de la
> pause descriptive, où un segment quelconque du discours narratif
> correspond à une durée diégétique nulle. (*DR,* p. 128)

In practice this freedom has, in the novelistic tradition as we know it,
been reduced to four basic speeds: *ellipse, sommaire, scène, pause.*

a) *Ellipse*

When a narrator employs ellipsis, he or she elides a certain amount
of narrative time, covers it in a zero amount of narrative (implicit
ellipsis) or in a very small segment of narrative (explicit ellipsis). With
implicit ellipsis, the narrator makes a temporal jump without explicitly
notifying the reader that he has done so. Genette cites the chronological
lacuna occurring between the end of *A l'ombre des jeunes filles en
fleurs* and the beginning of *Du côté de Guermantes:*

> nous savons que Marcel était rentré à Paris, où il avait retrouvé son
> 'ancienne chambre, basse de plafond'; nous le retrouvons dans un nouvel
> appartement dépendant de l'hôtel de Guermantes, ce qui suppose au moins
> l'élision de quelques jours, et peut-être sensiblement plus. (*DR,* p. 140)

The explicit ellipsis notifies the reader in a matter of a word or phrase

---

[14] See *Figures III,* pp. 126-7 for a fuller tabulation of narrative speeds in *A la recherche du temps
perdu.*

that a temporal jump has taken place. Temporal phrases such as 'deux jours plus tard' or 'quelques mois passèrent' offer the reader a coordinate, while at the same time consigning the intervening period to oblivion. However, as Michel Butor points out, reading habits tend to blind us even to these explicit signals:

> De temps en temps le récit procédera par flux, mais entre ces îlots de flux, nous ferons presque sans nous en douter d'énormes sauts. L'habitude nous empêche de faire attention à ces formules qui jalonnent les œuvres les plus filées, les plus coulantes: 'le lendemain...', 'quelque temps plus tard...', 'quand je le revis...'. (*op. cit.,* p. 116)

The ellipsis is clearly an economical device which allows the narrator to maintain a forward momentum and to pass over unimportant or irrelevant data. Sentences such as the following allow Maupassant to encompass within the restricted format of the short story a substantial period of time:

> Une année encore s'écoula, et il lui sembla qu'une nouvelle modification s'était accomplie dans l'esprit mystérieux du jeune homme. (*L'Orphelin*)

> Trois ans s'écoulèrent. (*Le Petit Fût*)

However, the ellipsis may not simply be a matter of narrative economy. It may also serve an important thematic function. The narrator's choice of an ellipsis may, for example, conceal a lack of important knowledge, a solipsistic perspective on what is happening around him, an attempt to repress unpleasant facts or a desire to deceive. Thus, in Gide's *La Porte étroite*, the last month of Alissa's life is elided in Jérôme's account of this period of his life. It is only Alissa's *Journal* which gives him painful and ironic access to the true nature of her feelings during this period.

b) *Sommaire*

The summary consists of the narration in a relatively short space of text of a relatively long period of time without providing detailed information about actions, exchanges of dialogue or description. In the nineteenth-century novel and indeed in most 'mimetic' fiction, the summary is the favourite device used to effect a transition between two scenes. The fundamental rhythm such fiction is based upon is an alternation between the summary and the scene. The summary is, as Genette points out, the background against which the scene is made to stand out:

> il est évident que le sommaire est resté, jusqu'à la fin du XIXe siècle, la
> transition la plus ordinaire entre deux scènes, le 'fond' sur lequel elles se
> détachent, et donc le tissu conjonctif par excellence du récit romanesque,
> dont le rythme fondamental se définit par l'alternance du sommaire et de la
> scène. (*DR*, p. 131)

Traditionally, most *analepses complétives* take the form of a summary
which briefly enumerates the salient or telling events of a character's
life. One should be wary, however, of simply taking such telescopic
surveys at face value. The summary is essentially a reductive device and
may imply a particular type of narratorial perspective, for example
humorous, critical, sympathetic, etc. The rapid-fire enumeration of
Candide's mishaps during his 'army training' prevents us from dwelling
upon their real horror and renders them farcical and unbelievable:

> On le fait tourner à droite, à gauche, hausser la baguette, remettre la
> baguette, coucher en joue, tirer, doubler le pas, et on lui donne trente coups
> de bâton; le lendemain, il fait l'exercice un peu moins mal, et il ne reçoit que
> vingt coups; le surlendemain, on ne lui en donne que dix, et il est regardé
> par ses camarades comme un prodige. (p. 59)

At the end of *L'Éducation sentimentale,* the résumé of Frédéric's life
between the sale of the Arnoux family property and his last encounter
with Madame Arnoux indicts his personality. It effectively reduces his
many and varied experiences to the status of discrete, aimless
enterprises reflecting his passivity, ineffectuality, and spinelessness:

> Il voyagea.
> Il connut la mélancolie des paquebots, les froids réveils sous la tente,
> l'étourdissement des paysages et des ruines, l'amertume des sympathies
> interrompues.
> Il revint.
> Il fréquenta le monde, et il eut d'autres amours encore. Mais le souvenir
> continuel du premier les lui rendait insipides; et puis la véhémence du désir,
> la fleur même de la sensation était perdue. Ses ambitions d'esprit avaient
> également diminué. Des années passèrent; et il supportait le désœuvrement
> de son intelligence et l'inertie de son cœur.[15]

In contrast, the terse, impersonal opening summary of Félicité's past in
Un Cœur simple brings out the limited horizons and pathos of her story:

> Elle avait eu, comme une autre, son histoire d'amour.
> Son père, un maçon s'était tué en tombant d'un échafaudage. Puis sa
> mére mourut, ses sœurs se dispersèrent, un fermier la recueillit, et
> l'employa toute petite à garder les vaches dans la campagne. Elle grelottait
> sous des haillons, buvait à plat ventre l'eau des mares, couchait sur la paille,
> servait les domestiques, à propos de rien était battue et finalement fut
> chassée pour un vol de trente sols, qu'elle n'avait pas commis.[16]

---

[15] *L'Éducation sentimentale,* ed. C. Gothot-Mersch (Paris: Garnier-Flammarion, 1985), p. 500.

[16] *Trois contes,* ed. P.M. Wetherill (Paris: Garnier Frères, 1988), p. 159.

Like the ellipsis, the summary may be disingenuous and reflect the narrator's ignorance, his desire to repress or his intention to deceive. In Gide's *L'Immoraliste,* Michel explicitly represses the details of memories which frighten him:

> Pourquoi parler des premiers jours? Qu'en reste-t-il? Leur affreux souvenir est sans voix. Je ne savais plus ni qui ni où j'étais. Je revois seulement, au-dessus de mon lit d'agonie, Marceline, ma femme, ma vie, se pencher. Je sais que ses soins passionnés, que son amour seul, me sauvèrent. Un jour enfin, comme un marin perdu qui aperçoit la terre, je sentis qu'une lueur de vie se réveillait; je pus sourire à Marceline. Pourquoi raconter tout cela? L'important, c'était que la mort m'eût touché, comme l'on dit, de son aile. (p. 29)

Later in his account he shows a similar reluctance to confront the details of his illness, preferring to concentrate upon his physical progress:

> Je ne parlerai pas de chaque étape du voyage. Certaines n'ont laissé qu'un souvenir confus; ma santé, tantôt meilleur et tantôt pire, chancelait encore au vent froid, s'inquiétait de l'ombre d'un nuage, et mon état nerveux amenait des troubles fréquents; mais mes poumons du moins se guérissaient. (p. 58)

In Michel Butor's *L'Emploi du temps,* it becomes clear that the most scrupulous narrator will find that he has taken liberties with 'real' time in narration. As events whose origins and causes lie in shadowy, unnoticed corners of the past begin to overtake Revel, he is forced to re-evaluate apparently minor details which he had neglected or falsified:

> J'ai donc lu dans la nuit d'hier ce récit que j'ai écrit moi-même, mais qui m'apparaissait de plus en plus comme l'œuvre scrupuleuse d'un autre à qui je n'aurais su confier qu'une partie de mes secrets, par manque de temps, par incapacité de distinguer encore tout ce qui était important, et aussi, je dois l'avouer par le desir de le tromper, cet autre, de me tromper moi-même.
>
> Car si je retrouvais dans ces pages quantité de détails que j'avais oubliés ou déformés, il n'en est pas moins vrai que je possédais encore toujours à ce sujet un certain nombre de renseignements que je n'y avais point notés, sans doute pour la plupart parce qu'ils se tenaient alors dans l'ombre, et que ce sont les événements qui ont suivi qui les en ont arrachés. (p. 195)

c) *Scène*

In the *scène dialoguée* or dramatic scene, there is an approximate coincidence between the duration of the fictional events and that of the narration. Obviously, the insertion of elucidative, attributive phrases such as 'dit-elle', 'répliqua-t-il' create minor discrepancies, but the direct account of the dialogue spoken by characters produces a close correlation between fictional time and the amount of text devoted to its coverage.

The dramatic scene is, generally speaking, an uneconomical way of conveying information. The narrator, in presenting ideas or character traits through dialogue, is attempting to 'show' rather than to 'tell' and requires at the same time much more deductive work on the part of the reader. Traditionally, the dramatic scene was used to mark key episodes of the story:

> Dans le récit romanesque tel qu'il fonctionnait avant la *Recherche,* l'opposition de mouvement entre scène détaillée et récit sommaire renvoyait presque toujours à une opposition de contenu entre dramatique et non dramatique, les temps forts de l'action coïncidant avec les moments les plus intenses du récit tandis que les temps faibles étaient résumés à grands traits et comme de très loin. [...] Le vrai rythme du canon romanesque, encore très perceptible dans *Bovary,* est donc alternance de sommaires non dramatiques à fonction d'attente et de liaison, et de scènes dramatiques dont le rôle dans l'action est décisif. (*DR,* p. 142)

The English critic Percy Lubbock, whose seminal work *The Craft of Fiction* (1921) anticipates Genette's model, saw the scene as a means whereby information we may have already had about a character is crystallised in a climax, for example a confrontation, a confession, a confidence. Hence the dialogue tends to signal a turning-point in the narrative.[17]

In *L'Immoraliste,*[18] the long central debates between Ménalque and Michel form the thematic core of the text in that they bring together two conflicting moral positions and *modi vivendi.* Michel's debates with Ménalque constitute the main turning-point of the text and set him upon a course of action which is to have profound consequences for himself and Marceline. Furthermore, the contrast between Michel's full account of these debates and the relatively scant attention he pays to Marceline's comments provides a gauge of his relative interest in the two characters and his neglect of his wife's thoughts and words, since he prefers to rationalise the silences between them in a favourable, romantic fashion:

> De combien de silence déjà savait s'envelopper notre amour! C'est que déjà l'amour de Marceline était plus fort que les mots pour le dire... (p. 99)

Michel's expansiveness and readiness to communicate with Ménalque also contrast sharply with his reticence and reluctance to participate in Marceline's conversations with the little group of Arab boys whom she has befriended. Here, conversation is summarised in the vaguest of terms as Michel refuses to acknowledge the nature of his own interest in them and his irritation at Marceline's presence:

---

[17] Compare Michel Butor, *op. cit.,* p. 118: 'On sent toute l'importance que pourraient avoir [...] les passages où il se produit une coïncidence entre la durée de la lecture et la durée de ce qu'on lit dans tous les dialogues, à partir desquels on pourra mettre en évidence précisément des ralentis ou des accélérations'.

[18] *Ibid.,* pp. 118-19.

> Elle me dit des noms; il y eut des questions, des réponses, des sourires, des moues, de petits jeux. [...] parler aux enfants, je ne l'osais pas devant elle. (p. 41)

d) *Pause*

With the description, the story effectively pauses though the narrative discourse carries on. The account of the succession of events is suspended while the narrator enumerates the features of a character or a place, or analyses the factors at work in a given situation. The description in Balzac tends to take the form of a set piece which interrupts the flow of the narrative and allows the narrator to set the scene, to draw attention to telling physical or psychological traits, or to explain the social situation. More subtly and less disruptively, the description may be distributed more evenly in the text and naturalised by reference to a character's own perception of or reaction to a scene. Thus the description of the landscape that may be viewed from the boat in the opening chapter of *L'Éducation sentimentale* is followed by Frédéric's fanciful and romantic reaction to it:

> Une plaine s'étendait à droite; à gauche un herbage allait doucement rejoindre une colline, où l'on apercevait des vignobles, des noyers, un moulin dans la verdure, et des petits chemins au delà, formant des zigzags sur la roche blanche qui touchait au bord du ciel. Quel bonheur de monter côte à côte, le bras autour de sa taille, pendant que sa robe balayerait les feuilles jaunies, en écoutant sa voix, sous le rayonnement des ses yeux! Le bateau pouvait s'arrêter, ils n'avaient qu'à descendre; et cette chose bien simple n'était pas plus facile, cependant, que de remuer le soleil! (pp. 53-4)

Furthermore, the passage has a pendant at the end of the novel in the account of Frédéric's last meeting with Madame Arnoux. Here, ironically he has the opportunity to realise his early fantasy, albeit in an urban setting, but remains too ineffectual to carry it through:

> au milieu des voitures, de la foule et du bruit, ils allaient sans se distraire d'eux-mêmes, sans rien entendre, comme ceux qui marchent ensemble dans la campagne, sur un lit de feuilles mortes. (p. 502)

The narrator's graphic comparison takes up and reworks the earlier description and commentary, thereby giving it a significant and integrative role in the structure of the novel.

The function of the description is clearly not limited to the information which it provides about the scene or character described. In many novels, the selection of data recorded reflects back upon the perceiver and his or her preoccupations and priorities. In *L'Immoraliste,* Michel's account of his journey back to Paris is

summarised and the great cities of European civilisation perfunctorily
dismissed, whereas his descriptions of Tunis and other southern towns
are lyrical and sensuous:

> Avant Ravenne, où nous nous attarderions donc quinze jours, nous
> verrions rapidement Rome et Florence, puis, laissant Venise et Vérone,
> brusquerions la fin du voyage pour ne nous arrêter plus qu'à Paris. (p. 77)

> Tunis. Lumière plus abondante que forte. L'ombre en est encore emplie.
> L'air lui-même semble un fluide lumineux où tout bouge,où tout baigne, où
> l'on plonge, où l'on nage. Cette terre de volupté satisfait mais n'apaise pas
> le désir, et toute satisfaction l'exalte.
>   Terre en vacance d'œuvres d'art. [...] Le peuple arabe a ceci
> d'admirable que, son art, il le vit, il le chante et le dissipe au jour le jour; il
> ne le fixe point et ne l'embaume en aucune œuvre. (pp. 174-5)

His descriptions of Bachir and Charles tell us less about them as
individuals than about Michel's ill-concealed sexual interest in them:

> Ses pieds sont nus; ses chevilles sont charmantes, et les attaches de ses
> poignets. [...] Ses cheveux sont rasés à la manière arabe; il porte une pauvre
> chéchia qui n'a qu'un trou à la place du gland. La gandourah, un peu
> tombée, découvre sa mignonne épaule. J'ai le besoin de la toucher. (p. 31)

> C'était un beau gaillard, si riche de santé, si souple, si bien fait [;...] à peine
> sa timidité ajoutait-elle encore à sa belle rougeur naturelle. Il semblait
> n'avoir que quinze ans, tant la clarté de son regard était demeurée enfantine.
> (p. 86)

The foregoing discussion makes it clear that the question of time in
fiction is not simply a thematic issue. It has considerable implications on
the level of structure which profoundly affect the reading strategy and
intelligibility. The highly sophisticated tools of analysis which have been
developed by structuralist critics have laid bare the conventions upon
which ostensibly 'mimetic' fiction has been founded, and shown the
extent to which temporal relationships have been reorganised,
telescoped, and weighted in the interests of 'good storytelling'. Genette's
model has also provided a crucial point of entry for the analysis of the
many experimental twentieth-century novels, whose intricacies of
construction and often radical deviation from nineteenth-century
conventions have proved difficult to accommodate critically. The
nouveau roman, for example, will frequently invert the temporal
conventions of traditional storytelling and deny the reader the
customary highlighting signals:

> L'idéal du récit quotidien, c'est, bien sûr, de ne retenir que l'important, le
> 'significatif', c'est-à-dire ce qui peut remplacer le reste, ce par quoi le reste
> est donné, et par conséquent de passer le reste sous silence, et même,
> procédant par degrés, de 's'attarder' sur l'essentiel et de 'glisser' sur le

secondaire. Mais un tel parallélisme entre la longueur occupée par un épisode et sa valeur significative est dans l'immense majorité des cas une pure illusion; un mot peut avoir des conséquences plus grandes qu'un long discours. Nous assisterons par conséquent à des inversions de structures. On pourra souligner l'importance de tel moment par son absence, par l'étude de ses alentours, faire sentir ainsi qu'il y a une lacune dans le tissu de ce qu'on raconte ou quelque chose que l'on cache.[19]

In focusing upon and showing the immense range of discrepancies between story-time and narrative time, Genette disallows facile impressionistic interpretation and establishes the identification of thematic priorities upon the meticulous examination of the temporal choices made by the narrator.

Clearly few readers have enough 'real' time to match Genette's fastidious study of Proust, but the discriminating reader should be aware of the extent to which fictional events are consciously ordered, integrated into significant patterns, and highlighted or discounted. The reader who neglects the order, frequencies and speeds of a text runs the risk of confusing story with truth, and could find himself to be the dupe of the disingenuous narrator. A warier reader will ask innumerable questions in the course of reading. The checklist which follows is proposed as a tentative and selective set of guidelines.

Narrative Time Checklist

Temporal Indications

1. How frequent are the temporal indications?

2. How precise are they?

3. Do the adverbs, conjunctions, tenses, allow you to relate periods/events to each other in chronological terms?

4. Do they distinguish clearly between past, present, and future?

5. Are they used consistently?

6. What is the temporal scope of the text or passage? Is it unusually narrow/unusually broad?

---

[19] Butor, *op. cit.*, pp. 118-19.

Ordre

1.   How faithful is the narrative to the chronological sequence of events? Identify disruptions in chronology.

2.   How conspicuous are the *analepses* and *prolepses* ? How are they signalled?

3.   How do they affect your understanding and interpretation? Is crucial information delayed? Are you given privileged information denied to characters?

4.   Do the *analepses* and *prolepses* serve an informative function? Or is their function primarily disruptive? Do they threaten the delivery of the story?

5.   At the end of the narrative can you reconstruct a coherent sequence of events?

6.   How do the *analepses* and *prolepses* relate to the central themes of the text? Do they, for example, challenge concepts such as determination, causality, intelligibility? Are they playful in intention? Do they expose and parody traditional methods of narrative construction?

Fréquence

1.   What is the dominant *fréquence* of a given text?

2.   If it is the *récit singulatif,* how are the events related to one another: by relationships of cause and effect, through parallelism, randomly? What do these relationships or lack of relationship indicate about the narrator's view of life and experience?

3.   If the dominant *fréquence* is the *récit répétitif,* is the repeated event described in precisely the same terms each time, or are there variations in expression? What is the significance of these variations? Is the repeated event recounted by different narrators? Do the accounts differ in style only, or are there differences of substance? Can you deduce a coherent common body of information? If there are discrepancies, what do they tell you about the various narrators? How do the discrepancies relate to or affect the general structure of the text?

4.   How prominent is the *récit itératif* ? Is it used as a narratorial
      short-cut to summarise a period of time? What does it tell you
      about the characters? Is their behaviour characterised by
      passivity, habit, obsession, etc.? What does the *récit itératif* tell
      you about the period covered? Does it do justice to the events
      related, or is it being used to control the information which you
      receive? Is its validity relativised by, for example, passages of
      récit singulatif?

Vitesses

1.   Are you given any indication(s) about the time-scale of the
      novel/story, section, chapter, paragraph, sentence?

2.   Is the narrative continuous, discontinuous?

3.   Compare and contrast the amount of fictional time covered by
      individual segments of texts. How conspicuous are the variations?

4.   Are certain periods omitted or drastically summarised? If so, is
      that the end of matter, or are they revealed to be important later
      in the text? Do we accept the narrator's distribution of emphasis?

5.   Do the summaries open out the limits of the narrative, put it in a
      broader context? Do they suggest more general (historical,
      philosophical, psychological, etc.) issues?

6.   Are the descriptive pauses conspicuous or discreet?
      Are there long chunks of description, or are the descriptive
      passages integrated into the text?

7.   Do the descriptive passages tell you more about the object of
      description or about the describer?

8.   Does the dialogue mark a climax or turning-point?
      Does it bring together previously developed strands of the
      fiction?
      Or is it apparently, trivial, banal? If so, does the apparent banality
      conceal undercurrents, sub-conversations?

9.   Does the dialogue constitute a revelation, a confrontation, a
      solution? Does it bring about change in the relationships of the
      characters?

10.   What do the variations in narrative speed tell you about the narrator's priorities, assumptions, intentions, reliability?

Exercises

1.   'L'auteur nous donne un résumé que nous lisons en deux minutes (qu'il a pu mettre deux heures à écrire), d'un récit que tel personnage aurait fait en deux jours, d'événements s'étalant sur deux ans' (Butor).

'Chacun sait qu'il n'est pas de roman pour si traditionnel et si 'réaliste' qu'il se présente, où le temps ne subisse des accélerations, des ralentissements, des coupures, des compressions, ou encore ce que l'on appelle de 'foudroyants raccourcis', c'est-à-dire qu'il est parfaitement *discontinu*' (Simon).

Discuss more fully the implications of these statements and find examples from your own reading of variations in narrative duration.

2.   To what extent is the concept of *fréquence* a thematically relevant issue in discussing the two-part structure of *L'Étranger?*

3.   Read the entries dated 'lundi 22 septembre' to 'mercredi 24 septembre' of Jacques Revel's diary (Michel Butor, *L'Emploi du temps*, pp. 290-6) and comment upon the narrative order.

4.   To what extent does Robbe-Grillet's novel *La Jalousie* both depend on and challenge the reader's expectations about narrative order?

5.   Compare and contrast the following summary in *Un cœur simple* of Madame Aubain's life with that of Félicité's life:

> Elle avait épousé un beau garçon sans fortune, mort au commencement de 1809, en lui laissant deux enfants très jeunes avec une quantité de dettes. Alors elle vendit ses immeubles, sauf la ferme de Toucques et la ferme de Geffosses, dont les rentes montaient à 5 000 francs tout au plus, et elle quitta sa maison de Saint-Melaine pour en habiter une autre moins dispendieuse, ayant appartenu à ses ancêtres et placée derrière les halles.

Chapter Five

S/Z and Narrative Codes

S/Z, Roland Barthes's seminal analysis of Balzac's novella *Sarrasine*, has generated considerable controversy among commentators. While pro-structuralist critics have claimed it as an exemplary application of structuralist methodology, others prefer to consider it in terms of a break with classical structuralism and Barthes's entry into the arena of deconstruction. In his book *On Deconstruction*, Jonathan Culler summarises both the structuralist and post-structuralist arguments:

> *S/Z* is very difficult to classify, not because it avoids the issues on which a distinction between structuralism and post-structuralism is generally based but because it seems to adopt both models with a vengeance, as though unaware that they are supposed to be radically different movements. *S/Z* displays a powerful metalinguistic drive: it seeks to break the literary work down into its constituents, naming and classifying them in a rationalist or scientific spirit; it identifies and describes the various codes on which the classical, readable text is based and explores at length the conventions of this mode of writing. [...] Yet at the same time, *S/Z* opens with what Barthes and others have regarded as a renunciation of the structuralist project: Barthes insists that rather than treat the text as the product or manifestation of an underlying system, he will explore its difference from itself, the way in which it outplays the codes on which it seems to rely.[1]

It is not our intention here further to fuel the controversy. Besides, Culler has demonstrated on more than one occasion that many of the key concepts of *S/Z* are to be found in Barthes's earlier work. What can be said with some certainty is that *S/Z* does herald a change of emphasis in that it attempts to analyse not the structure of literary texts, but what Coward and Ellis call their 'structuration', the dynamic process by which meaning is produced by both writer and reader.[2]

As we saw in Chapter Two, Barthes distinguishes between those texts which lend themselves fairly readily to naturalisation and those which strongly resist it. However, in establishing the twin poles of his theoretical model (the *lisible* and the *scriptible*), he adds a rider to the effect that no literary text is either completely *lisible* or completely *scriptible*. Thus the apparently rebarbative and incomprehensible text will eventually offer the reader some interpretive foothold, while the seemingly straightforward text, or one that has already been subjected to 'exhaustive' interpretation, will retain ambiguities and hints of obscurity.

---

[1] *On Deconstruction* (London and Henley: Routledge and Kegan Paul, 1983), p. 26.

[2] *Language and Materialism* (London: Routledge and Kegan Paul, 1977), p. 44.

If *S/Z* denies the critic the authority of definitive interpretation, it offers the reader a new, privileged role. *S/Z* should not be read as a work of criticism on Balzac; it is an instance of reading which plots the stages of meaning-production and reading strategy. The promotion of reading as an activity is a logical extension of structuralist interest in codes, the development of the concept of intertextuality, and the subversion of the notion of authorial originality. It must be understood that in Barthes's scheme of things the reader is not a distinctive, personalised individual, but a point of intersection of multiple codes and texts. The reader's subjectivity is not an inalienable psychological dimension, but a composite cultural product: 'La subjectivité est une image pleine, dont on suppose que j'encombre le texte, mais dont la plénitude, truquée, n'est que le sillage de tous les codes qui me font, en sorte que ma subjectivité a finalement la généralité même des stéréotypes' (*S/Z*, p. 17). For Barthes, the reader is, then, not an identifiable human being; rather he is an anonymous co-producer.

The task of the reader in interpreting the text is not to impose a single meaning, nor it is to personalise or appropriate it. Interpretation, Barthes insists, is to appreciate the plurality of the text's meanings:

> Lire, c'est trouver des sens, et trouver des sens, c'est les nommer; mais ces sens nommés sont emportés vers d'autres noms; [...] c'est une nomination en devenir, une approximation inlassable. (*S/Z*, p. 17)

Reading and interpretation are for Barthes a meticulous, graduated process, motivated and directed by the desire to name, to categorize, at least provisionally, the data encountered in the text. As the reader progresses through the text, his provisional labels and interpretive hypotheses will give way to other labels and hypotheses that will permit a greater accommodation of new data. Ultimately, reading is a potentially limitless approximative and revisionary process. It does not exhaust the text or lead to interpretive closure; it involves the adoption of a ludic attitude, a willing entry into the play of meaning upon meaning. It is this ludic dimension of reading which, Barthes argues, accounts for the activity of rereading, an activity which runs counter to contemporary habits of consumption. For the serious reader, the familiarity of the story and the knowledge of the outcome of fictional events are irrelevant; his interest lies with the interaction of vying elements and the inevitable revision, reversal, and multiplication of initial readings and interpretations. Reading, like play, is by definition an activity involving repetition and variation.

Barthes's promotion of pluralism and polysemy in the opening pages of *S/Z* seems to offer the reader no clear foothold for a practical analysis of an empirical text. Furthermore, Barthes could be charged with failing to distinguish between justifiable and unjustifiable interpretations. However, his sweeping generalisations relate to an ideal

reading of a hypothetical *scriptible* text. These remarks are qualified by
statements of a more pragmatic nature which acknowledge that reading
effectively slows down or puts a brake on the bewildering and unceasing
semantic play taking place within the text. Barthes goes on to elaborate
on the mechanisms by which this semantic play is slowed down. The
reader gains provisional purchase upon the text by dividing it into lexia
or reading units of varying length—whole sentences, phrases, individual
words. The fragmentation of the text into lexia is an heuristic strategy,
guided by the fact that each lexis has one or several identifiable
functions to play in the creation of meaning. The lexia are then analysed
in relation to the codes on which they depend for the meaning. These
codes do not have a fixed content which can then be tabulated; they are
mobile, evolving networks of allusion, referring the reader back to 'ce
quelque chose qui a toujours été déjà lu, vu, fait, vécu' (*S/Z*, p. 28).
Barthes explains the way in which the codes function by an analogy with
the 'voice off': 'Latéralement à chaque énoncé, on dirait que des voix
off se font entendre: ce sont les codes'(*ibid.*). The effect of their
combination is to detach the 'énoncé' from its origin; the text becomes a
space criss-crossed by impersonal voices which echo but do not
reproduce that which has already been written.

Barthes identifies and describes the remit of five codes—the
proairetic, the *hermeneutic,* the *referential,* the *semic,* and the
symbolic. Of these, the *proairetic,* despite its rather rebarbative label, is
the easiest to understand. The proairetic code relates to the process by
which the reader synthesizes and 'blocks out' data into sequences which
can then be given a name. In some cases the author will effectively do
this element of the reader's work by an unambiguous division of the text
into chapters and the supply of clear chapter titles (for example, in
Roger Martin du Gard's *Jean Barois,* 'Le docteur et sa mère au chevet
de Jean'; 'Entretiens de Jean avec l'abbé Schertz, sur les difficultés
religieuses'; 'Retour de Jean à Buis pour la mort de son père'). In other
cases, the reader will have to perform this task himself, gathering
together a certain amount of information under certain headings such as
'Promenade'; 'Assassinat'; 'Rendez-vous'. The function of this activity is
primarily pragmatic: it permits the reader to organise and reduce a
great deal of often diverse material into manageable units, thereby
facilitating critical allusion and discussion. In experimental modern
fiction, and in particular in the *nouveau roman,* this activity is rendered
deliberately problematical. Thus, in Robbe-Grillet's novel *La Jalousie,*
not only do the headings listed at the end of the novel fail to tell the
reader anything concrete about the 'content' of sections, but the
definitive identification of sequences is pre-empted by multiple internal
inconsistencies in chronology and the proliferation of variants and
alternative versions of conversations and scenes.

Barthes's explanation of the *hermeneutic* code is rather fuller and more complex. Like the proairetic code, the hermeneutic code relates to plot. However, the hermeneutic code may well work against the proairetic in that it contributes not to the establishment of sequences and chronology, but to the creation of suspense or mystery. The reader who wishes to make an inventory of the hermeneutic elements of the text will have to distinguish clearly between chronological indicators and the devices 'au gré desquels une énigme se centre, se pose, se formule, puis se retarde et enfin se dévoile' (*S/Z*, p. 26). The creation of suspense may consist simply of asking fairly crude 'whodunnit' types of questions, but it may also involve the posing of more sophisticated abstract problems of a moral, psychological, or philosophical order. Thus, Gide's *récit L'Immoraliste* opens with a triple problem explicitly formulated in the letter written by Michel's interlocutor: the nature of the change that has taken place in Michel's personality, the reasons for that change and the moral problem which his tale poses to others:

> Ce n'était plus le puritain très docte de naguère, aux gestes maladroits à force d'être convaincus, aux regards si clairs que devant eux souvent nos trop libres propos s'arrêtèrent. C'était... mais pourquoi t'indiquer déjà ce que son récit va te dire. (p. 12)

> [Les nouvelles] que Silas et Will, qui l'avaient revu, nous donnèrent, n'avaient pu que nous étonner. Un changement se produisait en lui, que nous n'expliquions pas encore. (p. 12)

> Ah! que vas-tu penser de notre ami? D'ailleurs qu'en pensé-je moi-même?... Le réprouverons-nous simplement, niant qu'on puisse tourner à bien des facultés qui se manifestent cruelles? (p. 10)

Whatever the nature of the question, suspense depends on the delay of the 'truth' of a matter or situation, while the reader's interest is maintained by the distribution throughout the text of clues or elements whose significance is not immediately apparent. The hermeneutic elements of the text structure its reading. Not only does it give the reader a sense of purpose and direction, but it requires the reader to organise data into combinations which 'make sense' and which reveal a meaning which is not present in individual elements.

The hermeneutic code will often be at work from the outset of the reading process. The title of a poem, story or novel may well beg important questions. Titles such as *Le Blé en herbe, Le Rouge et le Noir, L'Étranger, Moderato cantabile* or *Le Pays où l'on n'arrive jamais* do not yield their meaning readily; they provide a highly problematical clue to interpretation which nags at the reader until he has established an interpretive hypothesis capable of revealing their relevance to their respective tales.

As far as the body of the text is concerned, Barthes proposes an outline of the stages by which mystery and suspense are, typically, built up. By his own admission this list of stages is not definitive, and he recognises that not all of these stages are necessarily present in any one text. The reader's isolation of the problem or enigma to be resolved may be facilitated by an explicit narratorial formulation, as in the case of *L'Immoraliste,* or by a more discreet indication. Camus's *La Peste* opens with an allusion to unspecified but unusual 'événements', the nature of which is revealed by graduated states in the course of Rieux's account:

> Les curieux événements qui font le sujet de cette chronique se sont produits en 194., à Oran. De l'avis général, ils n'y étaient pas à leur place, sortant un peu de l'ordinaire.

Here, Camus at once exploits and plays on the hermeneutic formulation, offering the reader an intriguing opening summary, which will prove, in retrospect, to have been a considerable understatement. In Alain-Fournier's *Le Grand Meaulnes,* the reference to a momentous result, followed by a brief allusion to the cause, establishes in the reader's mind an unformulated connection which he can only elucidate by reading on:

> Mais quelqu'un est venu qui m'a enlevé à tous ces plaisirs d'enfant paisible. Quelqu'un a soufflé la bougie qui éclairait pour moi le doux visage maternel penché sur le repas du soir. Quelqu'un a éteint la lampe autour de laquelle nous étions une famille heureuse, à la nuit, lorsque mon père avait accroché les volets de bois aux portes vitrées. Et celui-là, ce fut Antoine Meaulnes, que les autres élèves appelèrent bientôt le grand Meaulnes.[3]

Thereafter, according to Barthes, the process by which the enigma is resolved will vary enormously according to the sophistication of the text, the complexity of the question, and the play of significance. By and large, however, the hermeneutic code works against the chronological flow of the story and operates through the distribution of *retards,* which hinder recuperation by the reader. Typically, the solution to the mystery will be graduated in the following manner. The formulation of the enigma may be followed by a *promesse de réponse,* an indication by the narrator that a solution will eventually be given. Such an indication clearly establishes a firm contract between the narrator and reader, and creates quite specific expectations in the latter. The faith of the reader in the contract, however, may have to weather certain *contretemps.* Before access to the 'truth' is conceded, the reader may well encounter a number of obstacles such as the *leurre* (an interpretive trap, false clue, piece of misleading information), the *équivoque* (a mixture of genuine and misleading information which, even if it allows more specific definition of the mystery, intensifies rather than elucidates it), the

---

[3] *Le Livre de Poche* (1971 [Mercure de France, 1902]), pp. 21-2.

blocage (an apparent blind alley or substantial impediment which confounds earlier hypotheses) and a *réponse suspendue* (an interruption in the elucidation of the mystery). Having traversed this interpretive obstacle course, the reader's patience will, if he is reading a classical text, normally be rewarded, but not necessarily immediately. A *réponse partielle* will at one and the same time permit a glimpse of the light at the end of the tunnel and prolong the journey, thereby delaying further the ultimate *dévoilement* or revelation.

The *referential* code consists of the body of accepted knowledge and cultural stereotypes which the reader brings to the text and on which the ideology, assumptions and generalisations of the text are based. The exploitation of elements from the referential code is one of the means by which an impression of verisimilitude is conferred upon the fictional world evoked. For obvious reasons, realist fiction relies particularly heavily upon the referential code. Balzac's attempt to classify humanity depends upon the assumption that cultural stereotypes and generalisations have an empirically verifiable currency value. He therefore resorts repeatedly to the referential code in order to confer an air of authority upon his analysis and to bolster the 'reality effect' of his narrative. Marcel Pagnol develops this reliance upon acquired knowledge into an important theme in *Jean de Florette,* one that exposes both the narrow-mindedness of time-honoured 'sagesse' and the dangers of modern 'science'. Jean invests all his hopes in the mastery of nature that the scientific manual promises him, and fails to take account of the possibility of humanly-engineered disaster:

> —Les chiffres sont là! dit le bossu. Il est vrai que ces 52 centimètres contiennent les pluies d'hiver. [...] Mais voici ce qui nous est dû par le ciel pour les mois de végétation: Avril, six jours de pluie. Mai, cinq jours. Juin, quatre jours. Juillet, deux jours. Août, trois. Septembre, six jours. Octobre, six jours.[4]

> —Voilà, expliqua le planteur, le secret de la végétation tropicale: après une pluie insistante et pénétrante, un grand coup de soleil stimule l'activité des tiges et des feuiles, en accélérant les échanges. Ce merveilleux système d'alternance vient de s'installer cet été. (p. 211)

Meanwhile, Papet looks to the oral tradition of proverb and superstition to bolster his confidence in his own schemes:

> *S'il pleut pour la Saint-Paterne,*
> *L'été sèche ta citerne.*

> *S'il pleut le jour de l'Ascension*
> *Tout s'en va en perdition.*

---

[4] *Jean de Florette* (Paris: Éditions de Fallois, 1988), p. 142.

> *S'il pleut en juin,*
> *Mange ton poing.*
>
> *S'il ne pleut pas pour Sainte-Anne,*
> *N'espère que Sainte-Jeanne.*[5]

and the townspeople use the axiom to justify their own culpable non-intervention in the underhand well-blocking activities of Papet and Ugolin:

> Ça ne rapporte jamais rien de s'occuper des affaires des autres. (p. 241)

Pagnol, in *Jean de Florette,* carries out a moral critique of certain types of inherited or derivative knowledge by punctuating his characters' speech with clichés, maxims and proverbs.

In *S/Z,* Barthes draws attention to Balzac's heavy reliance upon the referential code, arguing that the narration seems constantly to be referring the reader to a huge, anonymous and hypothetical book, a kind of multidisciplinary school manual that offers axiomatic statements on all of human life:

> Car d'une part, ce Livre antérieur est à la fois livre de science (d'observation empirique) et de sagesse, et d'autre part, le matériel didactique qui est mobilisé dans le texte [...] correspond à peu près au jeu des sept ou huit manuels dont pouvait disposer un honnête élève de l'enseignement classique bourgeois: une Histoire de la Littérature [...], une Histoire de l'Art [...], un manuel d'Histoire [...], un précis de Médecine pratique [...], un traité de Psychologie [...], un abrégé de Morale [...], une Logique [...], une Rhétorique et un recueil de maximes et proverbes concernant la vie, la mort, la souffrance, l'amour, les femmes, les âges, etc. (*S/Z,* p. 211)

Thus Balzac's prose is littered with axiomatic statements, proverbs, and illustrative analogies. These generalising figures of speech frequently serve to endorse characterisation, the representation of human relationships, or the logic of plot construction:

> Les gens généreux font de mauvais commerçants. (*Illusions perdues,* p. 16)

> Lucien avait au plus haut degré le caractère gascon, hardi, brave, aventureux, qui s'exagère le bien et amoindrit la mal, qui ne recule point devant une faute s'il y a un profit et qui se moque du vice s'il s'en fait un marchepied. (*Illusions perdues,* p. 31)

> Entre personnes sans cesse en présence, la haine et l'amour vont toujours croissant: on trouve à tout moment des raisons pour s'aimer on se haïr mieux.[6]

---

[5] For these four citations, see *Jean de Florette,* pp. 209; 209; 210; 218, respectively.

[6] *Le Curé de Tours,* Gallimard 'Folio' edition, pp. 58-9.

They may serve to impose a moral judgement:

> En conviant aujourd'hui tous ses enfants à un même festin, la Société
> réveille leurs ambitions dès le matin de la vie. Elle destitue la jeunesse de ses
> grâces et vicie la plupart de ses sentiments généreux en y mêlant des calculs.
> (*Illusions perdues*, p. 67)

or to reinforce verisimilitude by appealing to the reader's cultural
baggage, enlisting, for example, the support of a hypothetical specialist:

> Ce marteau, de forme oblongue et du genre de ceux que nos ancêtres
> nommaient jacquemart, ressemblait à un gros point d'admiration; en
> l'examinant avec attention un antiquaire y aurait retrouvé quelques indices
> de la figure essentiellement bouffonne qu'il représentait jadis, et qu'un long
> usage avait effacé.[7]

Balzac's notorious predilection for constructions based on
demonstratives plus relative clauses is another illustration of his
determination to nudge the reader into recognition and
acknowledgement of his fictional world through constant allusion to
'common knowledge' and 'experience of the world':

> Madame Grandet était [...] une de ces femmes qui semblent faites pour être
> tyrannisées. (*Eugénie Grandet*, p. 34)

> Lucien [...] était sur le point de prendre un de ces partis extrêmes auxquels
> on se décide à vingt ans. (*Illusions perdues*, p. 25)

It is precisely this sort of naive, positivist subscribing to general
principles which post-Einsteinian and post-Freudian critics and writers
have derided in Balzac. Ionesco and Beckett subvert the concepts of
knowledge and wisdom through nonsensical or contrary reformulations
of the proverb and axiom, while Claude Simon exposes and parodies the
strategies that in Balzac are used to create a cosy familiarity between
narrator and reader. Thus the 'Lexique' section of *La Bataille de
Pharsale* (1969) parodies Balzac's reliance on the demonstrative to
bridge the gap between his fictional world and the real world:

> [Les] formes [des nuages].sont celles que façonne un vent violent.

> La lumière a donc cette transparence et cette qualité [...] qui sépare
> nettement les formes.

> comme sur ces pistes de danse exiguës serrées entre les tables des soupeurs.

> comme ces animaux ou ces objets enfermés dans un bloc de plexiglas.

---

[7] *Eugénie Grandet*, Gallimard 'Folio' edition, p. 33.

comme ces chapeaux, ces coiffures, ces plissés, ces pourpoints, ces jabots
tuyautés, ces armures exagérément ornées.[8]

Most fiction, of course, falls somewhere between these two extremes.
Furthermore, reliance upon the referential code may well be
unacknowledged or even elaborately concealed. However, just as the
writer cannot avoid using the pre-existing *langue* in the formulation of
his *parole*, so too he cannot eliminate that which has already been said
or written from his own writing. The content of the referential code
(i.e. the body of general knowledge and assumptions) may change from
period to period, but it is here to stay and informs both writing and
reading in a very fundamental way. To ignore it is to disregard the
ideological perspective of both writers and readers and to court
accusations of dangerous naïveté.

Barthes's definition of the *semic* code is somewhat vague and
unsatisfactory, indeed circular:

> Pour les sèmes, on les relevera sans plus—c'est-à-dire sans essayer, ni de
> les tenir attachés à un personnage (à un lieu ou à un objet), ni de les
> organiser entre eux pour qu'ils forment un même champ thématique; on leur
> laissera leur instabilité, leur dispersion, ce qui fait d'eux les particules d'une
> poussière, d'un miroitement du sens. (*S/Z*, p. 26)

Fortunately, his practical analysis of the semic elements of the text is
rather more illuminating. In practice, this code seems to relate to the
distribution of *sèmes* or semantic features relating to character. The
reader, relying on psychological stereotypes, identifies elements in the
text which contribute to characterisation and tries to relate them to each
other. To clarify, Barthes isolates an example drawn from *Sarrasine:*

> Dire que Sarrasine est 'tour à tour agissant ou passif', c'est engager à
> repérer dans son caractère quelque chose 'qui ne prend pas', c'est engager à
> nommer ce quelque chose. (*S/Z*, p. 98)

The descriptive phrase which he isolates clearly creates a problem of
interpretation for the reader. It tells him what Sarrasine was like on
different occasions but it does not supply the name of a characteristic or
quality which would be applicable in all circumstances. Once again,
Barthes insists on the reader's urge to name and thereby to integrate the
character or characteristic within a coherent thematic frame of
reference:

> lire, c'est lutter pour nommer, c'est faire subir aux phrases du texte une
> transformation sémantique. (*S/Z*, pp. 98-9)

---

[8] *La Bataille de Pharsale* (Paris: Éditions de Minuit, 1969), pp. 101, 102, 103, 104, 105,
respectively

By way of illustration, he offers a selection of near-synonyms 'turbulent, trouble, instable, défait' which individually could be said to reduce the contradictory phrase to a single meaning.

Barthes's example and commentary illustrate what happens at the simplest level of reading. However, the reader is presented with many such interpretive problems in the course of reading an entire text. The naming of *sèmes* is a tentative and revisionary activity. As the reader proceeds through the text, he will often encounter new *sèmes* which, besides demanding to be named themselves, may well conflict with names and patterns established earlier in the reading. Reading thus proves to be an activity requiring great adaptability. The supply of a new name may simply require refinement upon the original interpretation; or else the reader may suddenly have to accommodate a new piece of information or an unexpected instance of behaviour which does not square with his original categories. In modernist, relativistic fiction, this particular reading problem is often given thematic prominence in its own right. In *A la recherche du temps perdu*, not only are the narrator and the reader repeatedly confronted with the problem of interpreting inconsistent behaviour, but the inconsistencies are such that they frequently fail to recognise (i.e. name) the characters concerned. Repeatedly the novels of Claude Simon and Nathalie Sarraute defy the reader to package and label characters by offering a superabundance of behavioural observations, epithets, and psychological explanations, many of which are incompatible and contradictory:

> Mais quel air renfrogné tout à coup, quelle moue dégoûtée... Quelle mouche le pique?... Ce petit ton sec qu'il prend pour refuser, ce regard moqueur... Il est plus accommodant d'ordinaire, moins timoré... Mais on ne sait jamais avec lui... Il suffit qu'il sente qu'elle en a tres envie... Ou bien c'est un manque subit de confiance en soi, un accès de sauvagerie, de paresse...[9]

Sarraute attacks the determinist and taxonomical approaches to psychology and inhibits the categorisation of characters, in her late novels, by refusing to identify narrators or to establish a hierarchy among explanations or labels, and by allowing free play to the pronouncements of multiple semic voices:

> Dans le texte moderne, les voix sont traités jusqu'au déni de tout repère: le discours, ou mieux encore, le langage parle, c'est tout. [...] La meilleure façon d'imaginer le pluriel classique est alors d'écouter le texte comme un échange chatoyant de voix multiples, posées sur des ondes différentes et saisies par moments d'un *fading* brusque, dont la trouée permet à l'énonciation de migrer d'un point de vue à l'autre, sans prévenir. (*S/Z*, pp. 48-9)

Given Barthes's self-confessed celebration of plurality and reading

---

[9] Sarraute, *Le Planétarium* (Paris: Gallimard, 'Folio', 1959), p. 21.

strategies which respect rather than reduce polysemy, the *symbolic* code
is in many respects the key to his approach. Its importance in the
analysis of a given text is in direct proportion to the intensity of
semantic play and depends upon a recognition on the part of the reader
of the difference between the empirical and the symbolic recuperation
of data. Empirical recuperation involves common sense and workaday
logic. It works on the assumption that a detail, action or event has a
cause which can be identified, and that the relationship between cause
and effect corresponds to our empirical experience of the world or to
the expectations inculcated in us by other books. Symbolic recuperation,
on the other hand, comes into play where empirically sufficient reasons
and causes are absent or fail fully to explain the emphasis given in a
particular text to a particular detail. Jonathan Culler illustrates the
difference between the two reading strategies by the following obvious,
but very clear examples:

> if a character's elegant dress is described we may call upon stereotyped
> models of personality and say that if he is so dressed it is *because* he is a
> fop or a dandy. (*SP*, p. 225)

> We would presumably be unwilling to assume a causal connection between
> a perfect or blemished complexion and a perfect or blemished moral
> character, but the symbolic code permits such associations and enables us to
> take the former as sign of the latter. Or again, there is no causal connection
> between moustaches and villainy but the symbolic code permits us to
> establish a sign relation. (*ibid.*)

The distinction between empirical and symbolic recuperation does
not usually pose a great problem. The establishment of acceptable
symbolic interpretations is another matter altogether, as both students of
literature and academic critics have frequently discovered to their cost.
Any attempt to establish a one-to-one equation between detail and
symbolic meaning is almost guaranteed to generate reproof,
qualification, or controversy. *S/Z* offers an alternative approach to the
symbolic which does not depend upon exhaustive scouring of
dictionaries of symbols, but which demands a more exactingly
systematic analysis of the specific text. Barthes argues that the symbolic
code functions through the establishment of a network of oppositions,
which prompt the attentive reader to recuperate the detail of the text in
terms of identifiable themes. Barthes's own analysis of *Sarrasine* centres
on Balzac's use of antithesis to invest his tale with resonances and
meanings which transcend and bind together its diverse elements. The
presentation of characters, events or detail in terms of a set of
oppositions forces the reader to look beyond the concrete, empirical
data of the story and calls upon him to integrate them into a symbolic
interpretation. The act of reading is oriented towards recuperation and

is motivated by the (often frustrated) desire to subsume the multiple
working hypotheses in a totalising symbolic interpretation. In order to
achieve a sense (or illusion) of control, the reader must hazard guesses,
albeit educated ones; he must try out various symbolic interpretations
until he finds one broad enough to satisfy him. Once again, Culler
offers a simple but illuminating example:

> The presentation of two heroines, one dark and the other fair, sets in motion
> an experiment in extrapolation in which the reader correlates this opposition
> with thematic oppositions that it might manifest: evil/good,
> forbidden/permitted, active/passive, Latin/Nordic, sexuality/purity. The
> reader can pass from one opposition to another, trying them out, even
> inverting them, and determining which are pertinent to larger thematic
> structures which encompass other antitheses presented in the text. (*SP*, pp.
> 225-6)

The obviousness of such oppositions will vary considerably from author
to author and from age to age. The oppositions which Balzac sets up
between Lucien Chardon and David Séchard in the first chapter of
Illusions perdues, and between Troubert and Birotteau in *Le Curé de
Tours,* are perceived by most modern readers as technically crude and
naive in their implicit determinism. The modernist writer will, on the
other hand, frequently set up a minefield of apparent oppositions, only
to subvert them ruthlessly. Thus, in his novel *Le Vent,* Claude Simon
establishes a number of thematic oppositions—good versus evil,
'grandeur de l'homme' versus 'misère de l'homme', passion versus
reason, stasis versus ephemerality, sensuality versus spirituality,
appearance versus truth, representation versus reality—all of which
give us some purchase on the text, but none of which offers a
satisfactory, totalising interpretation. Simon encourages us to follow up
each of these antithetical threads until we reach the inevitable impasse,
an impasse which is only breached when we recognise the overriding
thematic opposition: the tension between two different representational
codes, between traditional, realist conventions and Simon's exposure of
the tricks of the novelistic trade. In *Le Vent,* Simon sets the reader up
by investing the tale with a number of red herrings in the form of
recognisable thematic oppositions; however, in so setting him up, Simon
is also demonstrating that the erection and dismantlement of interpretive
hypotheses is a crucial factor in the appreciation of a text's plurality. In
the case of *Le Vent,* and indeed in most *nouveaux romans,* one can
ultimately 'close' the text within a general interpretive statement such as
'*Le Vent* is a self-conscious novel highlighting the problems and
conventions of writing'. However, as I have already argued elsewhere,
such a statement is unacceptably reductive, and underestimates the
attraction of the chase in favour of that of the kill.[10]

---

[10] See my article 'Antithesis in Simon's *Le Vent:* Authorial Red Herrings versus Readerly
Strategies', *The Modern Langue Review,* LXXXIII, 3 (July 1988), 571-85.

Meaning is, for Barthes, a subject which provokes both fascination and wariness. The natural tendency of meaning is to dominate, subjugate and subsume other meanings and its ability to do so depends upon the degree of its systematisation. Where a single meaning is allowed to dominate, it becomes ideology:

> Ainsi apparaît la nature du sens: c'est une force, qui tente de subjuguer d'autres forces, d'autres sens, d'autres langages. La force du sens dépend de son degré de systématisation: le sens le plus fort est le sens dont la systématisation englobe un nombre élevé d'éléments, au point de paraître recouvrir tout le notable du monde: ainsi des grands systèmes idéologiques, qui luttent entre eux à coups de sens. (*S/Z*, p. 160)

In the literary text, meaning is embodied in a *tissu de voix*, or network of codes. The more obviously systematic the organisation of this network is and the more readily compatible the references to these codes are, the closer the text comes to *lisibilité:*

> le discours s'enferme avec scrupule dans un certain cercle de *solidarités*, et ce cercle, où 'tout se tient', est celui du lisible. (*S/Z*, p. 162)

By contrast, the text which tends towards the *scriptible* subverts the establishment of a stable hierarchy of meanings and denies the reader the power to arrest the play of meaning:

> telle est bien la fonction de l'ecriture: rendre dérisoire, annuler le pouvoir (l'intimidation) d'un langage sur un autre, dissoudre, à peine constitué, tout métalangage. (*S/Z*, p. 105)

> Seule l'écriture, en assumant le pluriel le plus vaste possible dans son travail même, peut s'opposer sans coup de force à l'impérialisme de chaque langage. (*S/Z*, p. 212)

The reader who follows Barthes's models and who accepts his value system is committing himself to a paradoxical undertaking—he seeks to elucidate, recuperate, and reduce, but he hopes that he will never reach a point of final elucidation, recuperation, and reduction.

*****

I conclude this chapter with a preliminary codal analysis of Balzac's short story *La Messe de l'athée* (an abridged version of which follows), a brief checklist summary of points that may serve as an aid to practical application, and some suggested exercises.

La Messe de l'athée [1]

(abridged)

1: Un médecin à qui la science doit une belle théorie physiologique, et qui, jeune encore, s'est placé parmi les célébrités de l'École de Paris, centre de lumières auquel les médecins de l'Europe rendent tous hommage, le docteur Bianchon a longtemps
5   pratiqué la chirurgie avant de se livrer à la médecine. Ses premières études furent dirigées par un des plus grands chirurgiens français, par l'illustre Desplein, qui passa comme un météore dans la science. De l'aveu de ses ennemis,[4] il enterra dans la tombe une méthode intransmissible. Comme tous les gens de génie, il était sans
10   héritiers: il portait et emportait tout avec lui. La gloire des chirurgiens ressemble à celle des acteurs, qui n'existent que de leur vivant et dont le talent n'est plus appréciable dès qu'ils ont disparu. Les acteurs et les chirurgiens, comme aussi les grands chanteurs, comme les virtuoses qui décuplent par leur exécution la puissance
15   de la musique, sont tous les héros du moment. Desplein offre la preuve de cette similitude entre la destinée de ces génies transitoires.[5,6] Son nom, si célèbre hier, aujourd'hui presque oublié, restera dans sa spécialité sans en franchir les bornes.[3] [...] Desplein possédait un divin coup d'œil:[2] il pénétrait le malade
20   et sa maladie par une intuition acquise ou naturelle qui lui permettait d'embrasser les diagnostics particuliers à l'individu, de déterminer le moment précis, l'heure, la minute à laquelle il fallait opérer, en faisant la part aux circonstances atmosphériques et aux particularités du tempérament. Pour marcher ainsi de conserve
25   avec la Nature, avait-il donc étudié l'incessante jonction des êtres et des substances élémentaires contenues dans l'atmosphère ou que fournit la terre à l'homme qui les absorbe et les prépare pour en tirer une expression particulière? Procédait-il par cette puissance de déduction et d'analogie à laquelle est dû le génie de
30   Cuvier? [2] [...] Malheureusement tout en lui fut personnel: isolé dans sa vie par l'égoïsme,[5] l'égoïsme suicide aujourd'hui sa gloire.[7] Sa tombe n'est pas surmontée de la statue sonore qui redit à l'avenir les mystères que le Génie cherche à ses dépens. Mais peut-être le talent de Desplein était-il solidaire de ses croyances, et
35   conséquemment mortel.[8] [...] Desplein n'était pas dans le doute, il affirmait. Son athéisme pur et franc ressemblait à celui de beaucoup de savants, les meilleurs gens du monde, mais invinciblement athées, athées comme les gens religieux n'admettent pas qu'il puisse y avoir d'athées.[9] Cette opinion ne devait pas être
40   autrement chez un homme habitué depuis son jeune âge à disséquer l'être par excellence, avant, pendant et après la vie, à le fouiller dans tous ses appareils sans y trouver cette âme unique, si nécessaire aux théories religieuses. [...] Cet homme mourut, dit-on,

45 dans l'impénitence finale où meurent malheureusement beaucoup de
beaux génies, à qui Dieu puisse pardonner.[2, 10]

2: La vie de cet homme si grand offrait beaucoup de petitesses,
pour employer l'expression dont se servaient ses ennemis,[11] jaloux
de diminuer sa gloire, mais qu'il serait plus convenable de
nommer des contre-sens apparents.[12] N'ayant jamais connaissance
50 des déterminations par lesquelles agissent les esprits supérieurs, les
envieux ou les niais s'arment aussitôt de quelques contradictions
superficielles pour dresser un acte d'accusation sur lequel ils les
font momentanément juger.[13] [...]

3: Chez Desplein, la gloire et la science étant inattaquables,
55 ses ennemis s'en prenaient à son humeur bizarre, à son caractère;
tandis qu'il possédait tout bonnement cette qualité que les Anglais
nomment *excentricity*. Tantôt superbement vêtu comme Crébillon
le tragique, tantôt il affectait une singulière indifférence en fait de
vêtement; on le voyait tantôt en voiture, tantôt à pied. Tour à tour
60 brusque et bon, en apparence âpre et avare, mais capable d'offrir sa
fortune à ses maîtres exilés qui lui firent l'honneur de l'accepter[16]
pendant quelques jours, aucun homme n'a inspiré plus de jugements
contradictoires.[14, 15] [...] Chez un grand homme, les qualités sont
souvent solidaires. Si, parmi ces colosses, l'un d'eux a plus de talent
65 que d'esprit, son esprit est encore plus étendu que celui de qui l'on
dit simplement: Il a de l'esprit. Tout génie suppose une vue
morale.[17] [...]

4: Parmi les énigmes que présente aux yeux de plusieurs
contemporains la vie de Desplein, nous avons choisi l'une des plus
70 intéressantes, parce le mot s'en trouvera dans la conclusion du
récit, et le vengera de quelques sottes accusations.[18]

5: De tous les élèves que Desplein eut à son hôpital, Horace
Bianchon fut l'un de ceux auxquels il s'attacha le plus vivement.
Avant d'être interne à l'Hôtel-Dieu, Horace Bianchon était un
75 étudiant en médecine, logé dans une misérable pension du quartier
latin, connue sous le nom de la Maison Vauquer. Ce pauvre jeune
homme y sentait les atteintes de cette ardente misère, espèce de
creuset d'où les grands talents doivent sortir purs et incorruptibles
comme des diamants qui peuvent être soumis à tous les chocs sans
80 se briser.[19] [...] Horace était un jeune homme droit, incapable de
tergiverser dans les questions d'honneur, allant sans phrase au
fait, prêt pour ses amis à mettre en gage son manteau, comme à
leur donner son temps et ses veilles.[20] Horace était enfin un de ces
amis qui ne s'inquiètent pas de ce qu'ils reçoivent en échange de ce
85 qu'ils donnent, certains de recevoir à leur tour plus qu'ils ne

donneront. [...] Le grand Desplein disait tout à son interne;
l'interne savait si telle femme s'était assise sur une chaise auprès
du maître, ou sur le fameux canapé qui se trouvait dans le
cabinet et sur lequel Desplein dormait: Bianchon connaissait les
90 mystères de ce tempérament de lion et de taureau, qui finit par
élargir, amplifier outre mesure le buste du grand homme, et causa
sa mort par le développement du cœur. Il étudia les bizarreries de
cette vie si occupée, les projets de cette avarice si sordide, les
espérances de l'homme politique cachées dans le savant; il put
95 prévoir les déceptions qui attendaient le seul sentiment enfoui
dans ce cœur moins de bronze que bronzé.[21]

6: Un jour, Bianchon dit à Desplein qu'un pauvre porteur
d'eau du quartier Saint-Jacques avait une horrible maladie causée
par les fatigues et la misère; ce pauvre Auvergnat n'avait mangé
100 que des pommes de terre dans le grand hiver de 1821. Desplein
laissa tous ses malades. Au risque de crever son cheval, il vola,
suivi de Bianchon, chez le pauvre homme et le fit transporter
lui-même dans la maison de santé établie par le célèbre Dubois dans
le faubourg Saint-Denis. Il alla soigner cet homme, auquel il donna,
105 quand il l'eut rétabli, la somme nécessaire pour acheter un
cheval et un tonneau. Cet Auvergnat se distingua par un trait
original. Un de ses amis tombe malade, il l'emmène promptement
chez Desplein, en disant à son bienfaiteur: 'Je n'aurais pas
souffert qu'il allât chez un autre.' Tout bourru qu'il était, Desplein
110 serra la main du porteur d'eau, et lui dit: 'Amène-les-moi tous.' Et
il fit entrer l'enfant du Cantal à l'Hôtel-Dieu, où il eut de lui le plus
grand soin.[24] Bianchon avait déjà plusieurs fois remarqué chez son
chef une prédilection pour les Auvergnats et surtout pour les
porteurs d'eau; mais, comme Desplein mettait une sorte d'orgueil
115 à ses traitements de l'Hôtel-Dieu, l'élève n'y voyait rien de
trop étrange.[22, 25]

7: Un jour, en traversant la place Saint-Sulpice, Bianchon
aperçut son maître entrant dans l'église vers neuf heures du
matin. Desplein, qui ne faisait jamais alors un pas sans son
120 cabriolet, était à pied, et se coulait par la porte de la rue du
Petit-Lion, comme s'il fût entré dans une maison suspecte.
Naturellement pris de curiosité, l'interne [...] se glissa dans
Saint-Sulpice, et ne fut pas médiocrement étonné de voir le grand
Desplein, cet athée sans pitié pour les anges qui n'offrent point
125 prise aux bistouris, et ne peuvent avoir ni fistules ni gastrites,
enfin, cet intrépide *dériseur,* humblement agenouillé, et où?... à la
chapelle de la Vierge devant laquelle il écouta une messe, donna
pour les frais du culte, donna pour les pauvres, en restant sérieux

comme s'il se fût agi d'une opération.[23, 27]

130 **8:** —Il ne venait, certes, pas éclaircir des questions relatives à l'accouchement de la Vierge, disait Bianchon dont l'étonnement fut sans bornes. Si je l'avais vu tenant, à la Fête-Dieu, un des cordons du dais, il n'y aurait eu qu'à rire; mais à cette heure, seul, sans témoins, il y a, certes, de quoi faire penser!

135 **9:** Bianchon ne voulut pas avoir l'air d'espionner le premier chirurgien de l'Hôtel-Dieu, il s'en alla.[26] Par hasard, Desplein l'invita ce jour-là à dîner avec lui, hors de chez lui, chez un restaurateur. Entre la poire et le fromage Bianchon arriva, par d'habiles préparations, à parler de la messe, en la qualifiant de 140 momerie et de farce.

10: —Une farce, dit Desplein, qui a coûté plus de sang à la chrétienté que toutes les batailles de Napoléon et que toutes les sangsues de Broussais! La messe est une invention papale qui ne remonte pas plus haut que le VIe siècle, et que l'on a basée sur *Hoc* 145 *est corpus.* Combien de torrents de sang n'a-t-il pas fallu verser pour établir la Fête-Dieu par l'institution de laquelle la cour de Rome a voulu constater sa victoire dans l'affaire de la Présence Réelle, schisme qui pendant trois siècles a troublé l'Église! Les guerres du comte de Toulouse et les Albigeois sont la queue de 150 cette affaire. Les Vaudois et les Albigeois se refusaient à reconnaître cette innovation.

11: Enfin Desplein prit plaisir à se livrer à toute sa verve d'athée, et ce fut un flux de plaisanteries voltairiennes [...].

12: —Ouais! se dit Bianchon en lui-même, où est mon dévot de ce 155 matin?[28]

13: Il garda le silence, il douta d'avoir vu son chef à Saint-Sulpice. Desplein n'eût pas pris la peine de mentir à Bianchon: ils se connaissaient trop bien tous deux, ils avaient déjà, sur des points tout aussi graves, échangé des pensées, discuté des 160 systèmes *de natura rerum* en les sondant ou les disséquant avec les couteaux et le scalpel de l'Incrédulité.[29] Trois mois se passèrent. Bianchon ne donna point de suite à ce fait, quoiqu'il restât gravé dans sa mémoire. Dans cette année, un jour, l'un des médecins de l'Hôtel-Dieu prit Desplein par le bras devant Bianchon, comme 165 pour l'interroger.

14: —Qu'alliez-vous donc faire à Saint-Sulpice, mon cher maître? lui dit-il.[31]

15: —Y voir un prêtre qui a une carie au genou, et que madame
la duchesse d'Angoulême m'a fait l'honneur de me recommander,
170 dit Desplein.[32]

16: Le médecin se paya de cette défaite, mais non Bianchon.

17: —Ah! il va voir des genoux malades dans l'église! Il allait
entendre sa messe, se dit l'interne.[30]

18: Bianchon se promit de guetter Desplein; il se rappela le jour,
175 l'heure auxquels il l'avait surpris entrant à Saint-Sulpice, et se
promit d'y venir l'année suivante au même jour et à la même
heure, afin de savoir s'il l'y surprendrait encore. En ce cas,
la périodicité de sa dévotion autoriserait une investigation
scientifique, car il ne devait pas se rencontrer chez un tel homme
180 une contradiction directe entre la pensée et l'action. L'année
suivante, au jour et à l'heure dits, Bianchon, qui déjà n'était plus
interne de Desplein, vit le cabriolet du chirurgien s'arrêtant au coin
de la rue de Tournon et de celle du Petit-Lion, d'où son ami s'en
alla jésuitiquement le long des murs à Saint-Sulpice, où il entendit
185 encore sa messe à l'autel de la Vierge. C'était bien Desplein! le
chirurgien en chef, l'athée *in petto,* le dévot par hasard. L'intrigue
s'embrouillait. La persistance de cet illustre savant compliquait
tout.[34] Quand Desplein fut sorti, Bianchon s'approcha du sacristain
qui vint desservir la chapelle, et lui demanda si ce monsieur était un
190 habitué.

19: —Voici vingt ans que je suis ici, dit le sacristain, et depuis ce
temps monsieur Desplein vient quatre fois par an entendre cette
messe; il l'a fondée.

20: —Une fondation faite par lui! dit Bianchon en s'éloignant.
195 Ceci vaut le mystère de l'Immaculée Conception, une chose qui, à
elle seule, doit rendre un médecin incrédule.[33, 35]

21: Il se passa quelque temps sans que le docteur Bianchon,
quoique ami de Desplein, fût en position de lui parler de cette
particularité de sa vie. S'ils se rencontraient en consultation ou dans
200 le monde, il était difficile de trouver ce moment de confiance et de
solitude où l'on demeure les pieds sur les chenets, la tête appuyée
sur le dos d'un fauteuil, et pendant lequel deux hommes se disent
leurs secrets. Enfin, à sept ans de distance, après la révolution de
1830, quand le peuple se ruait sur l'Archevêché, quand les
205 inspirations républicaines le poussaient à détruire les croix dorées
que pointaient, comme des éclairs, dans l'immensité de cet océan de
maisons; quand l'Incrédulité, côte à côte avec l'Émeute, se carrait

dans les rues, Bianchon surprit Desplein entrant encore dans Saint-
Sulpice. Le docteur l'y suivit, se mit près de lui, sans que son ami
210 lui fît le moindre signe ou témoignât la moindre surprise. Tous
deux entendirent la messe de fondation.

22: —Me direz-vous, mon cher, dit Bianchon à Desplein quand
ils sortirent de l'église, la raison de votre capucinade? Je vous ai
déjà surpris trois fois allant à la messe, vous! Vous me ferez
215 raison de ce mystère, et m'expliquerez ce désaccord flagrant entre
vos opinions et votre conduite. Vous ne croyez pas en Dieu, et
vous allez à la messe! Mon cher maître, vous êtes tenu de me
répondre.

23: — Je ressemble à beaucoup de dévots, à des hommes
220 profondément religieux en apparence, mais tout aussi athées que
nous pouvons l'être, vous et moi.

24: Et ce fut un torrent d'épigrammes sur quelques personnages
politiques, dont le plus connu nous offre en ce siècle une nouvelle
édition du Tartufe de Molière.

225 **25:**—Je ne vous demande pas tout cela, dit Bianchon, je veux
savoir la raison de ce que vous venez de faire ici, pourquoi vous
avez fondé cette messe.

26: —Ma foi, mon cher ami, dit Desplein, je suis sur le bord de
ma tombe, je puis bien vous parler des commencements de ma
230 vie.[37] [...]

27: J'ai eu de si rudes commencements, mon cher Bianchon, que
je puis disputer à qui que ce soit la palme des souffrances
parisiennes. J'ai tout supporté: faim, soif, manque d'argent,
manque d'habits, de chaussure et de linge, tout ce que la misère a
235 de plus dur. [...] J'étais seul, sans secours, sans un sou ni pour
acheter des livres ni pour payer les frais de mon éducation
médicale; sans un ami; mon caractère irascible, ombrageux,
inquiet me desservait. Personne ne voulait voir dans mes
irritations le malaise et le travail d'un homme qui, du fond de
240 l'état social où il est, s'agite pour arriver à la surface. Mais j'avais,
je puis vous le dire, à vous devant qui je n'ai pas besoin de me
draper, j'avais ce lit de bons sentiments et de sensibilité vive qui
sera toujours l'apanage des hommes assez forts pour grimper sur
un sommet quelconque, après avoir piétiné longtemps dans les
245 marécages de la Misère. [...] Je voudrais bien voir l'un de ces
riches, qui se plaint que je lui prends trop cher quand il faut
l'opérer, seul dans Paris, sans sou ni maille, sans un

ami, sans crédit, et forcé de travailler de ses cinq doigts pour vivre? Que ferait-il? Où irait-il apaiser sa faim? Bianchon, si vous
250 m'avez vu quelquefois amer et dur, je superposais alors mes premières douleurs sur l'insensibilité, sur l'égoïsme desquels j'ai eu des milliers de preuves dans les hautes sphères; ou bien je pensais aux obstacles que la haine, l'envie, la jalousie, la calomnie ont élevés entre le succès et moi.[38] [...] Vous avez assez de talent, mon
255 cher enfant, pour connaître bientôt la bataille horrible, incessante que la médiocrité livre à l'homme supérieur. Si vous perdez vingt-cinq louis un soir, le lendemain vous serez accusé d'être un joueur, et vos meilleurs amis diront que vous avez perdu la veille vingt-cinq mille francs. Ayez mal à la tête, vous passerez pour un
260 fou. Ayez une vivacité, vous serez insociable. [...] Enfin vos qualités deviendront des défauts, vos défauts deviendront des vices, et vos vertus seront des crimes.[41] [...]

28: Vous savez! j'étais arrivé à l'une de ces dernières extrémités où l'on se dit: *Je m'engagerai!* [40] [...]

265 **29:** Enfin, je revins à la nuit, au moment où rentrait mon voisin, un porteur d'eau nommé Bourgeat, un homme de Saint-Flour. Nous nous connaissions comme se connaissent deux locataires qui ont chacun leur chambre sur le même carré, qui s'entendent dormant, toussant, s'habillant, et qui finissent par s'habituer l'un à
270 l'autre. Mon voisin m'apprit que le propriétaire, auquel je devais trois termes, m'avait mis à la porte: il me faudrait déguerpir le lendemain. Lui-même était chassé à cause de sa profession. Je passai la nuit la plus douloureuse de ma vie. 'Où prendre un commissionnaire pour emporter mon pauvre ménage, mes livres?
275 comment payer le commissionnaire et le portier? où aller?' Ces questions insolubles, je les répétais dans les larmes comme les fous redisent leurs refrains. [...] —Bah! j'ai quelques monnerons, Bourgeat me [...] dit joyeusement en me montrant une vieille bourse en cuir crasseux. Gardez votre linge. Bourgeat paya mes
280 trois termes, le sien, et solda le portier. Puis, il mit nos meubles, mon linge dans sa charrette, et la traîna par les rues en s'arrêtant devant chaque maison où pendait un écriteau. [...] Vers le soir, je découvris dans la cour de Rohan, passage du Commerce, en haut d'une maison, sous les toits, deux chambres séparées par l'escalier.
285 Nous eûmes chacun pour soixante francs de loyer par an. Nous voilà casés, moi et mon humble ami. Nous dînâmes ensemble. Bourgeat, qui gagnait environ cinquante sous par jour, possédait environ cent écus, il allait bientôt pouvoir réaliser son ambition en achetant un tonneau et un cheval. En apprenant ma situation, car il
290 me tira mes secrets avec [...] une bonhomie dont le souvenir me

remue encore aujourd'hui le. cœur, il renonça pour quelque temps à l'ambition de toute sa vie: Bourgeat était marchand à la voie depuis vingt-deux ans, il sacrifia ses cent écus à mon avenir.[42]

30: Desplein serra violemment le bras de Bianchon.

295 **31:** — Il me donna l'argent nécessaire à mes examens! Cet homme, mon ami, comprit que j'avais une mission, que les besoins de mon intelligence passaient avant les siens. [...] Le pauvre homme se sentait le cœur gros d'affections à placer; il n'avait jamais été aimé que par un caniche mort depuis peu de temps, et dont il me
300 parlait toujours en me demandant si je croyais que l'Église consentirait à dire des messes pour le repos de son âme. Son chien, disait-il, un vrai chrétien, qui, durant douze années, l'avait accompagné à l'église sans avoir jamais aboyé, écoutant les orgues sans ouvrir la gueule, et restant accroupi près de lui d'un air qui lui
305 faisait croire qu'il priait avec lui.[43] Cet homme reporta sur moi toutes ses affections: il m'accepta comme un être seul et souffrant; il devint pour moi la mère la plus attentive, le bienfaiteur le plus délicat, enfin l'idéal de cette vertu qui se complaît dans son œuvre. [...] Ce fut enfin le dévouement du peuple, l'amour de la grisette
310 reporté dans une sphère élevée. Bourgeat faisait mes commissions, il m'éveillait la nuit aux heures dites, il nettoyait ma lampe, frottait notre palier; aussi bon domestique que bon père, et propre comme une fille anglaise. Il faisait le ménage. Comme Philopémen, il sciait notre bois, et communiquait à toutes ses actions la simplicité du
315 faire, en y gardant sa dignité, car il semblait comprendre que le but ennoblissait tout.[44] [...] Dans la dernière année de mon internat, j'avais gagné assez d'argent pour rendre tout ce que je devais à ce digne Auvergnat en lui achetant un cheval et un tonneau. Il fut outré de colère de savoir que je me privais de mon
320 argent, et néanmoins il était enchanté de voir ses souhaits réalisés.[45] [...] Le pauvre homme s'était exterminé pour moi: il n'avait mangé que du pain frotté d'ail, afin que j'eusse du café pour suffire à mes veilles. Il tomba malade. J'ai passé, comme vous l'imaginez, les nuits à son chevet, je l'ai tiré d'affaire la première fois; mais il eut
325 une rechute deux ans après, et malgré les soins les plus assidus, malgré les plus grands efforts de la science, il dut succomber. Jamais roi ne fut soigné comme il le fut. Oui, Bianchon, j'ai tenté, pour arracher cette vie à la mort, des choses inouïes. Je voulais le faire vivre assez pour le rendre témoin de son ouvrage, pour lui
330 réaliser tous ses vœux, pour satisfaire la seule reconnaissance qui m'ait rempli le cœur, pour éteindre un foyer qui me brûle encore aujourd'hui![39]

32: —Bourgeat, reprit après une pause Desplein visiblement
ému, mon second père est mort dans mes bras, me laissant tout
335 ce qu'il possédait par un testament qu'il avait fait chez
un écrivain public, et daté de l'année où nous étions venus
nous loger dans la cour de Rohan. Cet homme avait la foi du
charbonnier. Il aimait la sainte Vierge comme il eût aimé une
femme. Catholique ardent, il ne m'avait jamais dit un mot sur mon
340 irréligion. Quand il fut en danger, il me pria de ne rien
ménager pour qu'il eût les secours de l'Église. Je fis dire
tous les jours la messe pour lui. Souvent, pendant la
nuit, il me témoignait des craintes sur son avenir, il
craignait de ne pas avoir vécu assez saintement. Le pauvre homme!
345 il travaillait du matin au soir. A qui donc appartiendrait le paradis,
s'il y a un paradis? Il a été administré comme un saint qu'il était, et
sa mort fut digne de sa vie. Son convoi ne fut suivi que par moi.
Quand j'eus mis en terre mon unique bienfaiteur, je cherchai
comment m'acquitter envers lui; je m'aperçus qu'il n'avait ni
350 famille, ni amis, ni femme, ni enfants. Mais il croyait! il avait une
conviction religieuse, avais-je le droit de la discuter? Il m'avait
timidement parlé des messes dites pour le repos des morts, il ne
voulait pas m'imposer ce devoir, en pensant que ce serait faire
payer ses services. Aussitôt que j'ai pu établir une fondation, j'ai
355 donné à Saint-Sulpice la somme nécessaire pour y faire dire quatre
messes par an. Comme la seule chose que je puisse offrir à
Bourgeat est la satisfaction de ses pieux désirs, le jour où se dit
cette messe, au commencement de chaque saison, j'y vais en son
nom, et récite pour lui les prières voulues. Je dis avec la bonne foi
360 du douteur: 'Mon Dieu, s'il est une sphère où tu mettes après leur
mort ceux qui ont été parfaits, pense au bon Bourgeat; et s'il y a
quelque chose à souffrir pour lui, donne-moi ses souffrances, afin
de le faire entrer plus vite dans ce qu'on appelle le paradis.' Voilà,
mon cher, tout ce qu'un homme qui a mes opinions peut se
365 permettre. Dieu doit être un bon diable, il ne saurait m'en vouloir.
Je vous le jure, je donnerais ma fortune pour que la croyance de
Bourgeat pût m'entrer dans la cervelle.[36, 46]

33: Bianchon, qui soigna Desplein dans sa dernière maladie, n'ose
pas affirmer aujourd'hui que l'illustre chirurgien soit mort athée.
370 Des croyants n'aimeront-ils pas à penser que l'humble Auvergnat
sera venu lui ouvrir la porte du ciel, comme il lui ouvrit jadis la
porte du temple terrestre au fronton duquel se lit: *Aux grands
hommes la patrie reconnaissante!* [47, 48, 49]

Paris, janvier 1836

Analysis of Narrative Codes
in *La Messe de l'athée*

1.	Title	Hermeneutic: a paradox, apparent contradiction in terms, which arrests the reader's attention and intrigues him.
2.	lines 1-5, 19-30, 35-45. 'Un médecin [...] la médecine.' 'Desplein possédait [...] Cuvier?' 'Desplein n'était [...] pardonner.'	Symbolic: science versus religion, i.e. one of the great debates of the nineteenth century. The first paragraph presents Desplein as a resolutely atheistic man of science, whose meticulous scientific investigations had given him no cause whatsoever to believe in an after-life or a soul. Here, the emphasis is on the deductive, rational and analytical procedures of science. However, there are one or two points which should raise doubt in the reader's mind, for example the phrasing of the sentence relating to the source of his genius. The use of the word 'divin' in 'Desplein possédait un divin coup d'œil' introduces at an early stage the possibility that his talent was god-given.
3.	lines 7-18 'Desplein, qui [...] les bornes.'	Symbolic: the eternal versus the ephemeral. The first paragraph dwells at some length on the fact that Desplein's reputation and knowledge died with him. This can be seen as typical Balzacian sleight of hand, a way of increasing the 'effet de réalité'. The fact that the reader has not heard of him does not mean that he did not exist. Balzac is, in effect, claiming that this is a 'true story'. However, these remarks have an important thematic function: the fact that Desplein's fame does not live on after him offers a parallel to his own lack of belief in a spiritual life.
4.	line 8 'De l'aveu de ses ennemis.'	Symbolic: reputation versus truth, appearance versus reality. Desplein's enemies are the origin of the rumour that his knowledge died with him.

5.	lines 16-17, 30-31 'génies transitoires.' 'isolé [...] gloire.'	Semic: the label 'génie transitoire' sums up Desplein's fate. The rest of the paragraph seems to confirm this view and to explain it. One of the reasons why his glory was so short-lived was that he was 'isolé dans son égoïsme'. Furthermore, it would seem that since he was an atheist, he was also excluded from spiritual rewards.
6.	lines 13-17 'Les acteurs [...] transitoires.'	Referential: the narrator establishes a long comparison between actors and surgeons on the basis of the ephemeral nature of their glory.
7.	lines 30-31 'isolé [...] gloire'.	Symbolic: selfishness versus generosity. In the first paragraph, the narrator makes a fairly dogmatic statement about Desplein which would seem to label him as an egotist: 'malheureusement, tout en lui fut personnel: isolé dans sa vie par l'égoïsme, l'égoïsme suicide aujourd'hui sa gloire.'
8.	lines 33-35 'Mais peut-être [...] mortel.'	Symbolic: eternal versus ephemeral. An implicit parallel is set up between the mortality of Desplein's genius and his lack of belief in an after-life.
9.	lines 36-39 'Son athéisme [...] y avoir d'athées.'	Referential: these lines bring together two apparently conflicting codes— atheism and religion. The point made here (i.e. that the religious do not have a monopoly on goodness) anticipates the relativistic tendency of the rest of the tale.
10.	lines 43-45 'Cet homme [...] pardonner.'	Symbolic: reputation versus truth, appearance versus reality. Again, the inclusion of the reference to hearsay ('dit-on') raises a doubt over the validity of the statement.
11.	line 47	Symbolic: reputation versus truth, appearance versus reality. Again, the

	'pour employer [...] ses ennemis.'	insertion of phrases signalling hostile sources alerts the reader to the possibility that, despite the fairly overwhelming evidence against Desplein, these statements are not truth, but opinion.
12.	lines 46-49 'La vie de [...] contre-sens apparents.'	Semic. The second paragraph takes up the contradiction implicit in the label 'génie transitoire'. Desplein was 'grand', but he also had 'beaucoup de petitesses'. However, this paragraph also introduces notes which raise some doubt about the dogmatism of the opening judgments. The phrases 'contresens apparents' and 'contradictions superficielles' suggest that there is more than meets the eye. These are the labels with which the reader must now work.
13.	lines 49-53 'N'ayant jamais [...] juger.'	Referential. The doubts raised about Desplein's reputation are strengthened by a general commentary on human nature.
14.	lines 49, 54-63 'N'ayant jamais [...] jugements contradic- toires.'	The phrase 'contre-sens apparents' suggests that there is more than meets the eye to Desplein's behaviour. Lines 43-50 develop the notion of appearances and contradictions and give a seris of examples of his contradictory behaviour for which there is no obvious answer. The ground is being prepared for the biggest contradiction of all: 'la messe de l'athée'.
15.	lines 55-63 'son humeur bizarre [...] jugements contradictoires.'	Semic. Paragraph **3** takes up and develops the question of Desplein's contradictions. Here, his genius and expertise are countered by his 'humeur bizarre', his 'caractère'. The narrator gives further examples of contradictory behaviour: sometimes well-dressed, sometimes badly-dressed; sometimes brusque, sometimes genial, sometimes 'âpre et avare', sometimes very

generous. All of these features can be provisionally explained by the notion of eccentricity.

16.	lines 59-61 'Tour à tour [...] l'accepter.'	Symbolic: selfishness versus generosity. Already the references to Desplein's selfishness are being qualified. He may at times seem selfish, but he is capable of generosity: 'en apparence âpre et avare mais capable d'offrir sa fortune à ses maîtres exilés'.
17.	lines 63-67 'Chez un grand [...] vue morale.'	Referential. This axiomatic statement belongs to a long tradition of theories on 'genius', but in this context it cuts across the specific view that atheism and immortality are irreconcilable. The statement 'Tout génie suppose une vue morale' anticipates the revelation of Desplein's charitable acts.
18.	lines 68-71 'Parmi les énigmes [...] sottes accusations '	Hermeneutic. The narrator declares explicitly that the tale concerns an enigma, promises a solution, and gives the reader a very broad indication regarding the nature of the revelation: it will overturn the reputation which certain people have given Desplein.
19.	lines 77-80 'cette ardente [...] se briser.'	Referential. The introduction of Horace Bianchon is followed by a long generalisation on the poverty that such young men must suffer, and its effect on their moral development. This is not a digression; it anticipates the tale which Desplein will have to tell. Furthermore, Desplein's affection for a young man such as Bianchon reflects well on himself.
20.	lines 80-83 'Horace [...] veilles.'	Symbolic: selfishness versus generosity. The theme of generosity is also incarnated by Horace Bianchon, who is described as 'prêt pour ses amis à mettre en gage son manteau, comme à leur donner son temps et ses veilles'. His

		characterisation is a variation in minor on one of the central themes.
21.	lines 95-96 'ce cœur [...] bronzé.'	Hermeneutic. The phrase 'ce cœur moins de bronze que bronzé' makes the reader speculate about the story behind Desplein's 'galvanised' heart.
22.	lines 97-116 'Un jour [...] trop étrange.'	Proairetic. Desplein's gift to anonymous water carriers, and Bianchon's thoughts on this.
23.	lines 97-129 'Un jour [...] opération.'	Semic. These lines offer very specific and startling of examples of Desplein's eccentricity—his particular sympathy for water carriers and *Auvergnats;* the image of this 'intrépide dériseur' at mass and 'humblement agenouillé'.
24.	lines 101-112 'Au risque [...] plus grand soin.'	Symbolic: selfishness versus generosity. The account of Desplein's generosity to the anonymous water carrier is another incident which belies Desplein's reputation. Furthermore, we learn that this is not an isolated incident.
25.	lines 112-116 'Bianchon [...] trop étrange.'	Hermeneutic. These lines constitute a partial formulation of the mystery. Desplein's generosity has a very precise target: he is particularly generous towards water carriers and *Auvergnats.* This information focusses the reader's attention upon a specific eccentricity.
26.	Lines 117-136 'Un jour [...] s'en alla.'	Proairetic. Desplein's first (observed) visit to church, and Bianchon's reaction.
27.	lines 117-129 'Un jour [...] d'une opération.'	Hermeneutic. Desplein's visit to the church and participation in the mass constitute what Barthes would call an 'équivoque'. The mystery is intensified by the revelation of further eccentric behaviour, and doubt is cast over earlier information, in particular over Desplein's atheism and the intimacy of

		his relationship with Bianchon, from whom we were told (line 68) he kept no secrets.
28.	Lines 136-155 'Par hasard [...] matin?'	Proairetic. Bianchon's conversation with Desplein about the history of Christianity and, in particular, the mass.
29.	lines 138-161 'Entre la poire [...] l'Incrédulité.'	Hermeneutic. The account of Bianchon's and Desplein's discussion over lunch and Bianchon's reflections afterwards produce a 'blocage'. Desplein's out-spoken condemnation of the mass and his atheistic jokes cause Bianchon to doubt his own eyes. The mystery seems to have no solution.
30.	lines 163-173 'Dans cette année [...] se dit l'interne.'	Proairetic. Encounter of Bianchon and Desplein with a colleague, and Desplein's unsatisfactory answer to the colleague's questions.
31.	lines 166-167 '—Qu'alliez-vous [...] lui dit-il.'	Hermeneutic. The mystery is reasserted. The remarks of another colleague confirm that Bianchon was not hearing things.
32.	lines 168-170 'Y voir [...] Desplein.'	Hermeneutic. Desplein replies to his inquisitive colleague with a 'leurre'—misleading information.
33.	lines 180-196 'L'année suivante [...] incrédule.'	Proairetic. Desplein's second (observed) visit to church and Bianchon's conversation with the sacristan, which adds to our information but which does not elucidate.
34.	lines 174-188 'Bianchon [...] compliquait tout.'	Hermeneutic. The revelation that Desplein's visits are precisely timed, regular occurrences intensifies the mystery and suggests that they are determined by a very precise, but as yet obscure reason. The narrator draws attention explicitly to this second 'équivoque': 'L'intrigue s'embrouillait.

		La persistance de cet illustre savant compliquait tout.'
35.	lines 191-196 'Voici [...] incrédule.'	Hermeneutic. The sacristan's disclosure that Desplein founded the mass intensifies the mystery.
36.	lines 208-367 'Bianchon surprit [...] cervelle.'	Proairetic. Encounter between Bianchon and Desplein at church, and conversation which elucidates. Note how the organisation of proairetic sequences has followed a regular pattern of observation followed by conversation. For the best part of the narrative, the discrepancy between the emerging pattern of behaviour and the conversation, between Desplein's actions and words, has widened. The gulf is bridged when Bianchon stops relying exclusively on empirical observation and deduction, and participates in the mass himself. It is only then that Desplein gives him access to the 'truth'.
37.	lines 228-230 '—Ma foi [...] ma vie.'	Hermeneutic. With the phrase 'Ma foi...', the solution of the mystery begins. However, it is a prolonged disclosure. The story Desplein tells is as important as the solution, since it takes up many of the antitheses already established in the text and subverts many of our general assumptions about his character. The creation of a mystery is to a large extent a means of maintaining the reader's interest while the themes of reputation versus truth, selfishness versus generosity, etc., are developed.
38.	lines 233-254 'J'ai tout supporté [...] succès et moi.'	Semic. In his own account of himself, Desplein acknowledges his rebarbative character, his 'caractère irascible, ombrageux, inquiet', but argues that this is the surface impression only. This appearance conceals a real depth of emotion and generosity, a 'lit de bons sentiments et de sensibilité'. It is also the

result of his treatment by other people, to whom a whole catalogue of negative labels is now attached: 'l'insensibilité', 'la haine', 'l'envie', 'la jalousie', 'la calomnie'. Here, the curious description at the end of paragraph five ('ce cœur moins de bronze que bronzé' is expanded and explained. He is the victim of other people's malice. He is not 'avare', but the victim of the rich, who accuse him of charging too much. In the course of the narrative, then, the view of Desplein's personality is 'corrected', first by the qualification and then by the subversion of the initial labels applied to him. Not only is his 'égoïsme' undermined, but it is seen as being one of the features of his accusers.

| 39. | lines 233-332 | Symbolic: selfishness versus generosity. The account of Bourgeat's self-sacrifice is the most fully developed treatment of the theme of generosity in the tale. |
| | 'J'ai tout supporté [...] aujourd'hui!' | |

| 40. | lines 254-264 | Referential. Desplein's use of the referential code illustrates the way in which it acts as a context in which communication and understanding can take place. |
| | 'Vous avez [...] *Je m'engagerai!'* | |

| 41. | lines 255-262 | Symbolic: reputation versus truth, appearance versus reality. Desplein gives a host of examples of the ways in which people will take a fact and distort it. His remarks explain the reputation which he has acquired and suggest its tenuousness. |
| | 'la bataille horrible [...] des crimes.' | |

| 42. | lines 260-293 | Hermeneutic. The account of Bourgeat's kindness offers a partial solution to the mystery of Desplein's own generosity towards water carriers and *Auvergnats*. |
| | 'Enfin [...] mon avenir.' | |

| 43. | lines 297-305 | Hermeneutic. The reference to the dog owned by Bourgeat and his owner's wish that he could found a mass for it is a |
| | 'Le pauvre [...] | |

	avec lui ' 'leurre'. The reader, remembering Desplein's visits to the church and not knowing at this stage that Bourgeat is dead, may be inclined to think that Desplein had managed to found a mass for the dog. In fact, this account, although misleading, does anticipate the way in which Bourgeat is to be repaid.

44. lines 307-316

'il devint [...] ennoblissait tout.'

Referential. The greatest cluster of cultural references is to be found in the description of the many things which Bourgeat did for Desplein. Here, the range and multitude of references to cultural stereotypes translate the inability of Desplein to sum him up in a simple description of his qualities or by reference to one ideal type. His devotion can only be communicated by reference to a model case, but one such model is not enough. This proliferation of references is in many ways a paradoxical use of the referential code, which is a kind of ideological shorthand. The accumulation here makes the point that Bourgeat's generosity and self-sacrifice are truly exceptional.

45. lines 316-320

'Dans la dernière [...] souhaits réalisés '

Hermeneutic. Desplein's account of his gift of the horse and cart to Bourgeat effectively delays the revelation of his real way of repaying him. The similarity between this gesture and the earlier account of his generosity to an unknown water carrier suggests that this gift was not his final repayment of his huge debt to an exceptional man.

46. lines 333-367

'—Bourgeat, reprit [...] cervelle.'

Hermeneutic. Desplein's final speech solves the mystery of the mass. However, it is not a straightforward solution. Desplein had tried every means to find an earthly recompense, but Bourgeat has no relatives. The establishment of a mass was a last resort.

47.	lines 333-373	Symbolic: eternal versus ephemeral. The last two paragraphs bring the narrative back to the original judgment on Desplein's life and achievements. That judgment is challenged by the hypotheses that he may have abandoned his atheistic stance and that he may have gained access to eternal glory.
	'—Bourgeat, reprit [...] *reconnaissante.*'	
48.	lines 333-373	Semic. The last two paragraphs bring the narrative back to the title and initial commentary, and raise a question mark over both Desplein's atheism and the transitory nature of his glory. Nothing of the judgment which provided the starting-point for the narrative remains intact.
	'—Bourgeat, reprit [...] *reconnaissante.*'	
49.	lines 368-373	Hermeneutic. Having solved the two mysteries behind Desplein's actions and eccentric behaviour, the narrator raises, in the final lines, unanswerable questions about his spiritual state at the time of death, and the fate of his soul.
	'Bianchon [...] *reconnaissante.*'	

Conclusions

Note the way in which the final paragraphs bring together the various threads of the tale. On the level of the plot, a solution is given to the mystery which has been established in the course of the narrative. The characterisation of Desplein has involved numerous revisions, and finally a reversal of original premises. On the level of the symbolic code, all the thematic oppositions are brought into play and re-examined by the conclusion.

Eternal versus ephemeral: Not only does Desplein recognise the limits of secular knowledge (he fails to cure Bourgeat), but he is unable to find a suitable reward in this world for Bourgeat's sacrifice. He has to resort to a spiritual solution which presupposes heavenly rewards. Furthermore, Bianchon's remarks raise a question mark over the view that Desplein died an atheist—i.e., he may have achieved eternal life after all.

Science versus religion: Even if Desplein did not die a Christian, his account of his attempt to reward Bourgeat reveals a yearning to believe: 'Je vous le jure, je donnerais ma fortune pour que la croyance de Bourgeat pût m'entrer dans la cervelle'. Desplein has come as near to believing as the doubting man of science can. It is both amusing and very moving that he should formulate what is really a prayer in terms of a hypothesis: 'Je dis avec la bonne foi du douteur: "Mon Dieu, s'il est une sphère où tu mettes après leur mort ceux qui ont été parfaits, pense au bon Bourgeat; et s'il y a quelque chose à souffrir pour lui, donne-moi ses souffrances, afin de le faire entrer plus vite dans ce qu'on appelle le paradis"'. In short, the science/religion opposition is attenuated, becomes a question of the discrepancy between doubt and speculation.

Selfishness versus generosity: This opposition has already been greatly relativised in the course of the tale, but there are a couple of further developments in the conclusion. Desplein's reward to Bourgeat involves the sacrifice of his own principles. In asking God to give Bourgeat's suffering to him so that the water carrier can go to paradise, Desplein is showing a willingness to accept the rules of a God, in whom he apparently does not believe.

Reputation versus truth: The final development in the treatment of this thematic opposition comes with the revelation that Desplein has in fact concealed his greatest act of generosity. He has the ability to reverse the general view of himself, but does not. He is clearly far from being the egotist he is taken for.

Narrative Codes Checklist

1. Referential Code

Look out for explicit indications of the narrator's assumptions, such as:

aphorisms, maxims, proverbs.
clichés.
comparisons (in particular, those based on the formula ' [comme] un de ces [...] qui').
statements of opinion.
explicit addresses to the reader.
references to other forms of writing, representation; allusions to texts with which, it is assumed, we are familiar.

2. Proairetic Code

Identify the broad units, episodes of the narrative and try to label them.
Do these units correspond to chapter divisions, or do they run over?
Do these units cover similar or widely differing periods of fictional
time?
Are they of roughly equal or widely discrepant textual lengths?
Are they self-contained units, or are their limits fluid?
Does the narrator give clear indications of the limits of these units (e.g.
chapter headings, summaries, etc.)?

3. Hermeneutic Code

Barthes has identified a number of stages in the construction of plot, in
particular in the establishment, development and resolution of some kind of
mystery. In your reading of narrative, try to bear Barthes's scheme in
mind. Look for the following:

la thématisation: emphatic indication of the enigmatic subject.
la position: indications(s) that we are dealing with the 'enigmatic genre'.
la formulation de l'énigme: statement of the nature of the enigma.
la promesse de réponse: indication that a solution will eventually be
given.
le leurre: a trap, false clue, something which misleads.
l'équivoque: an ambiguity which intensifies the mystery or increases the
suspense.
le blocage: an impediment or admission of defeat, declaration that the
mystery is insoluble.
la réponse partielle: partial solution.
le dévoilement: revelation.

4. Semic Code

How quickly can you apply a set of labels to the characters?
Does the narrator supply a set of labels? Are these labels appropriate,
reliable? Are you working with, or against the narrator?
Do the labels tell you more about the character or about the narrator?
Is the narrator judgemental, naive, cynical, etc.?
Does the character's behaviour in the rest of the text correspond to your
initial labels? Do you have to revise them as you read?
How often do you have to revise them? (a) only after major events,

developments? Or (b) frequently (because of the inconsistency of the character's behaviour, new information, the diverse opinion of other characters, etc.)?

Are you able to resolve contradictions, inconsistencies in your information about the characters?

Can you establish a definitive label or set of labels at the end of the narrative, or does the character resist interpretation to the end?

5. Symbolic Code

Try to identify thematic oppositions within the text.

Are these oppositions familiar or unexpected?

Are they stark or are they qualified, ambiguous?

Are they explicitly formulated, or does the reader have to extrapolate?

Does the writer make use of antithesis as a stylistic device?

How many oppositions can you identify? Is there a pattern underlying them? Are they related thematically to one another?

Do the oppositions remain constant throughout the text? Are they qualified, undermined in the course of the text?

Exercises

1. Our analysis here is based on an abridged version of *La Messe de l'athée*. Carry out a similar analysis of the entire text. The most accessible edition is *Balzac: Short Stories*, edited by A.W. Raitt (Oxford University Press: 'Clarendon French Series', 1964).

2. Write an essay on the operation of the symbolic code in any work of fiction that you are currently studying.

3. Read the description of the Pension Vauquer at the beginning of Balzac's novel *Le Père Goriot* and comment on the use of the referential code.

Conclusion

In this guide, I hope to have provided an insight not only into the theory and practice of structuralism, but also into the complexity of the issues begged by the literary text. Structuralist analysis reveals again and again that even those texts which have been apparently exhausted by criticism are underpinned by conventions and paradigms which only a detailed, systematic approach can expose. The reader who neglects these conventions and paradigms takes substantial risks: in particular, he is in danger of confusing nature and art, truth and text, and of remaining unaware of the multiple and often devious ways in which the text is manipulating him. An understanding of the artifice of the text will not only result in the clearer identification of formal devices; it will also encourage a sharper critical approach to 'familiar' classics and provide a point of entry to more recent, often apparently rebarbative and irrecuperable texts. The theoretical models outlined here represent only a small fraction of the body of critical methodology developed by structuralists. It is hoped that these models will have proven useful and enlightening, and that students will use the guide as the basis for further enquiry into a complex but rewarding field. The bibliography which follows offers a selection of introductory commentaries, theoretical works and critical studies which should facilitate future research.

Bibliography

For the sake of brevity, full bibliographical references that have already been given in footnotes are not reiterated here. Unless otherwise stated, works in English and French are published in London and Paris, respectively.

Barthes, R. 'Changing Views of Character', in *New Literary History,* vol, 5, no. 2 (1974).

Capitanio, S. '*La Bête humaine:* intratextualité et intertextualité', in *Zola: 'La Bête humaine': texte et explications,* actes du colloque de Glasgow, 1990 (Glasgow:University French and German Publications, 1990), pp. 100-122.

Chambers, R. *Meaning and Meaningfulness: Studies in the Analysis and Interpretation of Texts.* Lexington, KY: French Forum, 1979.

Chatman, S. *Story and Discourse: Narrative Structure in Fiction and Film.* Ithaca and London: Cornell U.P., 1978.

Cohan, S. & Shires, L. *Telling Stories, A Theoretical Analysis of Narrative Fiction.* New York and London: Routledge, 1988.

Combe, D. *Poésie et récit: une rhétorique des genres.* Corti,1989.

Coward, R. & Ellis, J. *Language and Materialism.* Routledge & Kegan Paul, 1977.

Duffy, J.H. 'Les Codes narratifs dans *Djinn* d'Alain Robbe-Grillet', *Degré second,* no. 10 (1986), 39-49.

'Narrative Code versus Truth: The Prosecution Case in *L'Étranger'*, *Essays in Poetics,* 14, 2 (1989), 18-42.

Hamon, P. 'Mise au point sur les problèmes de l'analyse du récit', *Le Français moderne,* 40 (1972), pp. 220-21.

Hawkes, T. *Structuralism and Semiotics.* Methuen, 1977.

Heath, S. *The 'Nouveau roman'.* Elek, 1972.

Imbert, P. *Sémiotique de la description balzacienne.* Ottawa: Éditions de l'Université d'Ottawa, 1978.

Jefferson, A. & Robey, D (eds.). *Modern Literary Theory: A Comparative Introduction.* Batsford, 1986 (revised edition).

Kadish, D.Y. 'Alissa dans la vallée: Intertextual Echoes of Balzac in Two Novels by Gide', *French Forum,* vol. 10, no. 1 (1985), pp. 67-83.

Lane, M. (ed.)   *Structuralism: A Reader.* Jonathan Cape, 1970.

Lavers, A.   *Structuralism and After.* Methuen, 1982.

Lodge, D.   *Working with Structuralism, Essays and Reviews on Nineteenth-and Twentieth-Century Literature.* Routledge and Kegan Paul, 1981.

                   Modern Criticism and Theory: A Reader. Longman, 1988.

Martin, W.   *Recent Theories of Narrative.* Ithaca & London: Cornell University Press, 1986.

Mathews, T.   *Reading Apollinaire: Theories of Poetic Language.* Manchester: Manchester University Press, 1987.

Mileham, J.W.   *The Conspiracy Novel: Structure and Metaphor in Balzac's 'Comédie humaine'.* Lexington, KY: French Forum, 1982.

Mitterand, H.   *Le Discours du roman.* Presses Universitaires de France, 1980.

Pratt, T.M.   'Victor Hugo à la lumière de Roland Barthes', *Studi Francesi,* anno XXXIV, no. 101 (1990), 253-7.

Pettit, P.   *The Concept of Structuralism: A Critical Analysis.* Berkeley: University of California Press, 1975.

Prendergast, C.   *The Order of Mimesis.* Cambridge: Cambridge University Press, 1986.

Prince, G.   *Narratology: The Form and Functioning of Narrative.* Berlin, New York, Amsterdam: Mouton, 1982.

Rice, D. &   *Rhetorical Poetics.* Madison, WI: Univ. of Wisconsin Press, 1983.
Schofer, P. (eds.)

Rimman-   *Narrative Fiction: Contemporary Poetics.* Methuen, 1983.
Kenan, S.

Robey, D.   *Structuralism: An Introduction.* Oxford: Clarendon Press, 1973.

Scholes, R.   *Structuralism in Literature.* New Haven & London: Yale University Press, 1974.

                   Semiotics and Interpretation. New Haven & London: Yale University Press, 1982.

Selden, R.   *A Reader's Guide to Contemporary Literary Theory.* Brighton: Harvester Press, 1985.

Sturrock, J.   *Structuralism and since: from Lévi-Strauss to Derrida.* Oxford:
(ed.)   University Press, 1979.

Yücel, T.   *Figures et messages de la 'Comédie humaine'.* Mame, 1972.